Editor

Mary S. Jones, M.A.

Editor in Chief

Karen J. Goldfluss, M.S. Ed.

Cover Artist

Tony Carrillo

Imaging

James Edward Grace
Craig Gunnell

Publisher

Mary D. Smith, M.S. Ed.

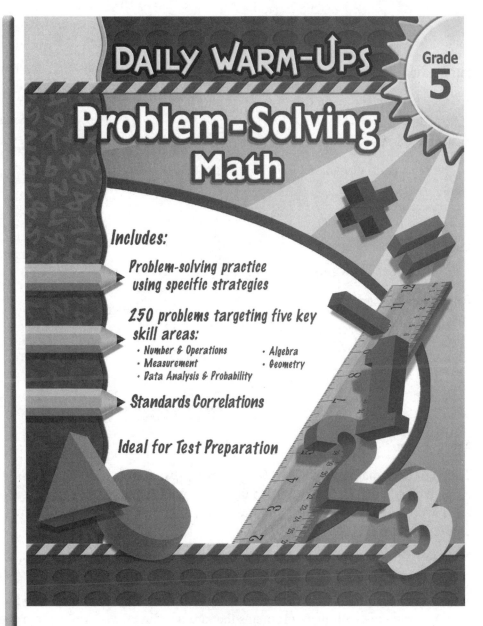

Daily Warm-Ups

Grade 5

Problem-Solving Math

Includes:

Problem-solving practice using specific strategies

250 problems targeting five key skill areas:
- Number & Operations
- Measurement
- Data Analysis & Probability
- Algebra
- Geometry

Standards Correlations

Ideal for Test Preparation

Author

Robert W. Smith

Teacher Created Resources

6421 Industry Way
Westminster, CA 92683
www.teachercreated.com

ISBN: 978-1-4206-3579-9

© 2011 Teacher Created Resources
Made in

D1504869

Teacher Created Resources

Table of Contents

Introduction

About this Book

The variety of math problems in *Daily Warm-Ups: Problem-Solving Math* will provide students with enough problem-solving practice to introduce your math period every day for an entire school year. For each warm-up, allow 10 to 15 minutes for reading, interpreting, and solving the problems before you correct them as a class.

Students can work on the problems in this book independently, in groups, or as a whole class. Decide which approach works best for your students, based on their math skill levels and reading competence.

The book is divided into two sections. The first section of the book introduces five specific problem-solving strategies with math problems that are not directly addressed to a specific operation or concept. The math strategies are as follows: Creating an Organized List, Guessing and Checking, Looking for a Pattern, Using Tree Diagrams, and Working Backwards. (See pages 8–12 for examples of math problems to which these types of strategies apply.) The second section of the book contains more traditional problems in operations, numeration, geometry, measurement, data analysis, probability, and algebra. The general math area and focus addressed in each warm-up is noted at the top of each page.

These activities can be used in a variety of ways, but they were designed to be introductory warm-ups for each math period. The 250 warm-ups are individually numbered and should be used in any order according to your main math lessons. Choose warm-ups that cover concepts previously taught so that the warm-up can serve as a review.

NCTM Standards

The math problems in this book have been correlated to the National Council of Teachers of Mathematics (NCTM) standards. See the correlation chart on pages 4–7. You will find the standards and expectations along with the warm-up numbers to which they relate. As the NCTM math standards make clear, problem solving is the critical component in math instruction. It is the component that makes general operations knowledge both essential and useful. Problem solving is the basic element in the concept of math as a method of communication.

Introduction *(cont.)*

Daily Warm-Ups, Section 1

The 50 warm-ups in this section follow one of five key problem-solving strategies. Each of these pages is set up the same way, allowing students to quickly become familiar with the expectations of the problems. The answers to the problems in this section have been provided along with explanations of the thinking process behind solving each one. (See pages 163–170 for Section 1's answers.)

Math strategy requested to solve the problem

Student's final answer(s) should be written here (if line is given)

Student's brief explanation of steps taken to solve problem (encourage use of math vocabulary)

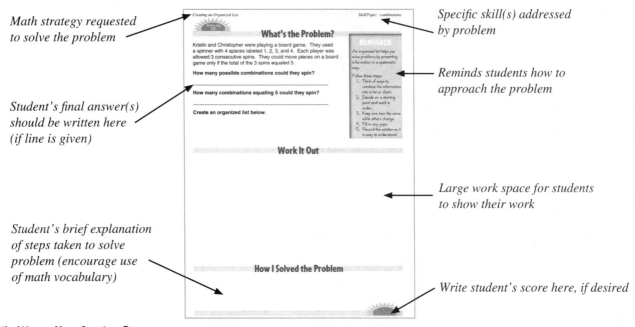

Specific skill(s) addressed by problem

Reminds students how to approach the problem

Large work space for students to show their work

Write student's score here, if desired

Daily Warm-Ups, Section 2

The 200 warm-ups in this section are divided into five math areas: Number and Operations, Geometry, Measurement, Data Analysis and Probability, and Algebra. Each of these pages has two warm-ups on the page. The two warm-ups relate to each other in some way. Warm-ups may be separated and given to students independently. However, in some cases, the top warm-up is needed in order to complete the bottom warm-up. Such pages are indicated with a chain symbol in the top right corner. These "linked" warm-ups should not be separated.

Math area and focus

Student's final answer(s) should be written here (if lines are given)

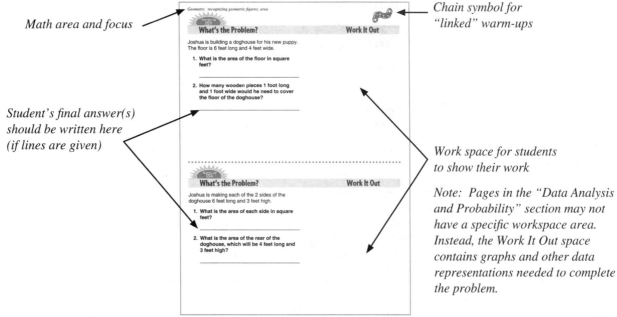

Chain symbol for "linked" warm-ups

Work space for students to show their work

Note: Pages in the "Data Analysis and Probability" section may not have a specific workspace area. Instead, the Work It Out space contains graphs and other data representations needed to complete the problem.

Correlation to NCTM Standards

The following chart lists the National Council of Teachers of Mathematics (NCTM) standards and expectations for grades 3–5. Reprinted with permission from *Principles and Standards for School Mathematics*. (Copyright 2000 by the National Council of Teachers of Mathematics. All rights reserved.)

Standards and Expectations	Warm-Up Numbers
NUMBER AND OPERATIONS	
Understand numbers, ways of representing numbers, relationships among numbers, and number systems	
• Understand the place-value structure of the base-ten number system and be able to represent and compare whole numbers and decimals	16, 67, 68
• Recognize equivalent representations for the same number and generate them by decomposing and composing numbers	3, 4, 17, 18
• Develop understanding of fractions as parts of unit wholes, as parts of a collection, as locations on number lines, and as divisions of whole numbers	165–168
• Use models, benchmarks, and equivalent forms to judge the size of fractions	73, 74
• Recognize and generate equivalent forms of commonly used fractions, decimals, and percents	50, 55, 56, 59, 60, 65, 66, 71–76, 79, 80, 86, 89, 90
• Explore numbers less than 0 by extending the number line and through familiar applications	241–244
• Describe classes of numbers according to characteristics such as the nature of their factors	51–54, 77, 78, 81, 82, 127, 128
Understand meanings of operations and how they relate to one another	
• Understand various meanings of multiplication and division	24, 26–28, 30, 51–54, 61, 62, 79–82, 85
• Understand the effects of multiplying and dividing whole numbers	19, 24, 26, 28, 30, 51–54, 61, 62, 81, 82
• Identify and use relationships between operations, such as division as the inverse of multiplication, to solve problems	51–54, 83, 84
Compute fluently and make reasonable estimates	
• Develop fluency with basic number combinations for multiplication and division and use these combinations to mentally compute related problems, such as 30×50	4, 12, 13, 16, 51–56
• Develop fluency in adding, subtracting, multiplying, and dividing whole numbers	1, 12, 13, 17, 20, 51–54, 61–64, 69, 70, 83, 84, 87, 88
• Develop and use strategies to estimate the results of whole-number computations and to judge the reasonableness of such results	9, 13–17, 19–21, 26, 46, 48, 50–52, 63, 64, 67, 68, 239, 240
• Develop and use strategies to estimate computations involving fractions and decimals in situations relevant to students' experience	12–14, 17, 18, 55–60, 65, 66, 71–76, 86–90
• Use visual models, benchmarks, and equivalent forms to add and subtract commonly used fractions and decimals	14, 57–60, 73, 74
• Select appropriate methods and tools for computing with whole numbers from among mental computation, estimation, calculators, and paper and pencil according to the context and nature of the computation and use the selected method or tools	1, 12, 16, 19, 26, 46, 67–70, 147, 148

Standards are listed with the permission of the National Council of Teachers of Mathematics (NCTM). NCTM does not endorse the content or validity of these alignments.

Standards and Expectations	Warm-Up Numbers
GEOMETRY	
Analyze characteristics and properties of two- and three-dimensional geometric shapes and develop mathematical arguments about geometric relationships	
• Identify, compare, and analyze attributes of two- and three-dimensional shapes and develop vocabulary to describe the attributes	49, 91–102, 105, 106, 109, 110, 119–124, 127, 128, 151, 152
• Classify two- and three-dimensional shapes according to their properties and develop definitions of classes of shapes such as triangles and pyramids	91, 92, 117–120, 123, 124
• Investigate, describe, and reason about the results of subdividing, combining, and transforming shapes	75, 76, 119, 120, 127
• Make and test conjectures about geometric properties and relationships and develop logical arguments to justify conclusions	75, 76, 117, 118, 127, 161, 162
Specify locations and describe spatial relationships using coordinate geometry and other representational systems	
• Describe location and movement using common language and geometric vocabulary	113–118, 123, 124, 127, 161, 162
• Make and use coordinate systems to specify locations and to describe paths	113–116, 129, 130, 209, 210
• Find the distance between points along horizontal and vertical lines of a coordinate system	113–116, 129, 130, 209, 210
Apply transformations and use symmetry to analyze mathematical situations	
• Describe a motion or a series of motions that will show that two shapes are congruent	115, 116
Use visualization, spatial reasoning, and geometric modeling to solve problems	
• Build and draw geometric objects	151, 152, 161–164
• Create and describe mental images of objects, patterns, and paths	75, 76, 97, 98, 103, 104
• Identify and build a three-dimensional object from two-dimensional representations of that object	95, 125, 126
• Identify and draw a two-dimensional representation of a three-dimensional object	103, 104, 125, 126
• Use geometric models to solve problems in other areas of mathematics, such as number and measurement	75, 76, 91–96, 99, 100, 105–108, 111, 112
• Recognize geometric ideas and relationships and apply them to other disciplines and to problems that arise in the classroom or in everyday life	75, 76, 91–100, 105–110
MEASUREMENT	
Understand measurable attributes of objects and the units, systems, and processes of measurement	
• Understand such attributes as length, area, weight, volume, and size of angle and select the appropriate type of unit for measuring each attribute	49, 91, 92, 101, 102, 107, 108, 135, 136
• Understand the need for measuring with standard units and become familiar with standard units in the customary and metric systems	93–96, 109–112, 135, 136, 141–143, 149, 150, 155, 156
• Carry out simple unit conversions, such as from centimeters to meters, within a system of measurement	131, 132, 141–143, 149, 150, 153–156, 169, 170

Standards and Expectations	Warm-Up Numbers
MEASUREMENT	
Understand measurable attributes of objects and the units, systems, and processes of measurement *(cont.)*	
• Understand that measurements are approximations and how differences in units affect precision	131, 132, 153, 154
• Explore what happens to measurements of a two-dimensional shape such as its perimeter and area when the shape is changed in some way	75, 76
Apply appropriate techniques, tools, and formulas to determine measurements	
• Select and apply appropriate standard units and tools to measure length, area, volume, weight, time, temperature, and the size of angles	49, 107–112, 137, 138
• Select and use benchmarks to estimate measurements	145, 146
• Develop, understand, and use formulas to find the area of rectangles and related triangles and parallelograms	95, 96, 99, 100, 103, 104, 106–108, 133, 134
• Develop strategies to determine the surface areas and volumes of rectangular solids	49, 109–112, 133, 134
DATA ANALYSIS AND PROBABILITY	
Formulate questions that can be addressed with data and collect, organize, and display relevant data to answer them	
• Collect data using observations, surveys, and experiments	171, 172, 186
• Represent data using tables and graphs such as line plots, bar graphs, and line graphs	21, 22, 26, 27, 47, 113, 114, 171–184, 189, 190
• Recognize the differences in representing categorical and numerical data	31, 165–168, 171–176, 179–182
Select and use appropriate statistical methods to analyze data	
• Describe the shape and important features of a set of data and compare related data sets, with an emphasis on how the data are distributed	5–8, 21, 22, 26–28, 30, 41, 171–176, 183–188
• Use measures of center, focusing on the median, and understand what each does and does not indicate about the data set	139, 140, 144, 157–160, 170, 207, 208
• Compare different representations of the same data and evaluate how well each representation shows important aspects of the data	24, 25, 27, 28, 37–41, 165–168, 185, 186, 191–194, 207, 208
Develop and evaluate inferences and predictions that are based on data	
• Propose and justify conclusions and predictions that are based on data and design studies to further investigate the conclusions or predictions	32–41, 43, 44, 171, 172, 185, 186, 197, 198
Understand and apply basic concepts of probability	
• Describe events as likely or unlikely and discuss the degree of likelihood using such words as certain, equally likely, and impossible	10, 32–40, 191–206
• Predict the probability of outcomes of simple experiments and test the predictions	10, 32, 33, 39, 40, 195–206
• Understand that the measure of the likelihood of an event can be represented by a number from 0 to 1	10, 191–202

Standards and Expectations	Warm-Up Numbers
ALGEBRA **Understand patterns, relations, and functions**	
• Describe, extend, and make generalizations about geometric and numeric patterns	2, 8, 28, 29, 31, 35, 40, 41–47, 213, 214
• Represent and analyze patterns and functions, using words, tables, and graphs	23–29, 31, 40–48
Represent and analyze mathematical situations and structures using algebraic symbols	
• Represent the idea of a variable as an unknown quantity using a letter or a symbol	21, 24, 211–228, 231–234, 245–250
• Express mathematical relationships using equations	211–226, 231–234, 237, 238
Use mathematical models to represent and understand quantitative relationships	
• Model problem situations with objects and use representations such as graphs, tables, and equations to draw conclusions	9, 11, 15, 22–27, 30–33, 41–46, 48, 50, 229, 230, 235–238, 247, 248
Analyze change in various contexts	
• Investigate how a change in one variable relates to a change in a second variable	10, 20–26, 29, 46, 47, 50, 69, 70, 223, 224, 229, 230, 249, 250
• Identify and describe situations with constant or varying rates of change and compare them	9, 15, 21–27, 29, 30, 45, 50, 221, 222, 225–228, 235–238

Examples of Strategies

Creating an Organized List

An organized list helps you solve problems by presenting information in a systematic way.

Follow these steps:

1. Think of ways to combine the information into a list or chart.

2. Decide on a starting point and work in order.

3. Keep one item the same while others change.

4. Fill in any gaps.

5. Record the solution so it is easy to understand.

Example 1

What's the Problem?

Carla has an orange hat and a yellow hat. She also has 3 scarves (purple, gray, and black).

How many different combinations of hats and scarves can she wear without repeating the same combination?

List the combinations.

Work It Out

	Hat	Scarf
1	orange	purple
2	orange	gray
3	orange	black
4	yellow	purple
5	yellow	gray
6	yellow	black

How I Solved the Problem

To solve the problem, a student would use the information given to fill in the first row of an organized list. To make the list effective, one variable (hat color) should remain the same until the other variable (scarf color) is used completely.

Example 2

What's the Problem?

Steve is learning how to speak Spanish. In the first week, he learned 8 Spanish words. Each week after that, he plans on learning 12 new Spanish words.

How many words will he know at the end of the 4th week?

How many weeks will it take him to learn over 150 words?

Work It Out

Week	New Words	Total Words
1	8	8
2	20	28
3	32	60
4	(44)	104
(5)	56	160

How I Solved the Problem

To solve the problem, a student would create a list using the information given. In the list, the column of new words increases by 12 each time, while the column of total words is the running total. Continue the list until the running total is greater than 150.

Examples of Strategies

Guessing and Checking

Guessing and checking helps you find reasonable guesses to solve a problem. For each guess, look at the important information presented in the problem. Check the guess against the information. Base the next guess on the previous result to see if your choices were too large or too small. (Recording your guesses and results in a chart or table also helps.) Repeat the steps until the problem is solved.

Example 1

What's the Problem?

Three players on Tom's football team, the Leopards, are among the league's leaders in receptions. Those 3 players have combined to catch 312 balls.

Which 3 players on the list of League Leaders are on the Leopards?

League Leaders

Name	Receptions
A. Jones	113
W. Blake	111
J. Rivers	106
R. Stone	102
P. Smith	100
L. Hand	93

Work It Out

```
  113        113        113
  111        100        106
+ 106      +  93      +  93
  330        306        312
```

Answer:	A. Jones	113
	J. Rivers	106
	L. Hand	93
		312

How I Solved the Problem

To solve the problem, a student would begin by guessing the answer and checking to see the result. A student might first add the 3 highest numbers to find out the total. From there, a student can make a more educated guess about which numbers to add.

Example 2

What's the Problem?

While cleaning, Craig found 15 total coins under his couch. Six of the coins were nickels. Combined, the quarters, dimes, nickels, and pennies he found totaled $1.38.

How many of each coin did he find?

Use the chart to solve the problem.

Work It Out

P	N	D	Q	Total
3	6	2	4	$1.53
3	6	4	2	$1.23
3	6	3	3	$1.38

How I Solved the Problem

To solve the problem, a student would begin by guessing an answer and recording the results in a table. Based on the information given, a guess can be made that either 3 or 8 pennies were found. From there, an educated guess can be made about the other coins.

Examples of Strategies

Looking for a Pattern

Looking for patterns makes it easier to predict what comes next. In a problem, study any number patterns to see how the numbers change from one number to the next. For example, to find the rule for the pattern, 2, 7, 22, 67, study how 2 and 7, 7 and 22 are related, etc. You will see that each number is 3 times the number before it plus 1, or (n x 3) + 1.

Example 1

What's the Problem?

Sam went to an all-day music festival on Saturday. Sam counted 100 people in attendance to watch the first band. By the time the second band played, he counted 140. There were 220 there to see the third band, and 380 there to see the fourth band.

If this pattern continued, how many people would be in attendance to watch the popular sixth band?

Work It Out

Band	People
1	100
2	140
3	220
4	380
5	700
6	(1340)

How I Solved the Problem

To solve the problem, a student would create a list to analyze the data. The student would first think about how the numbers 100 and 140 are related and then how 140 is related to 220. By doing this, the student can see that the pattern is that the number of people added each time doubles.

Example 2

What's the Problem?

Marathon runner Mike awards himself points for each mile he runs. He gives himself 5 points for the first mile, 10 points for the second mile, and 20 for the third mile. By the time he has run 5 miles, he has earned a total of 125 points.

Based on this pattern, how many points did he earn for the 6th mile?

If he runs a sixth mile, how many points will Mike have earned in total?

Work It Out

Mile	Points	Total
1	5	5
2	10	15
3	20	35
4	35	70
5	55	125
6	(80)	(205)

How I Solved the Problem

To solve the problem, a student would create a list to analyze the data. The student would first think about how the numbers 5, 10, and 20 are related and what the total of those numbers would be. By doing this, the student can see that the pattern is that the number of points added is 5 more than were added to the previous mile.

Examples of Strategies

Using Tree Diagrams

Create a tree diagram to show how the different items in a problem are connected. This strategy is helpful for solving problems where you need to find all possible combinations of the items. Begin by organizing a list of the items. Link each item into a tree diagram until all possible combinations are shown. Use the results to help solve the problem.

Example 1

What's the Problem?

Frank flipped a quarter 3 times to see if it would come up heads or tails.

How many different possible outcomes can result from flipping a coin 3 times?

Work It Out

1st Flip	2nd Flip	3rd Flip

```
1st Flip        2nd Flip        3rd Flip

                   H ───────────── H
        H ──────<                 
                   T ───────────── T
                          H ────── H
                                    T
                   H ───────────── H
        T ──────<                 
                   T ───────────── T
                          H ────── H
                                    T
```

There are 8 possible outcomes.

How I Solved the Problem

To solve the problem, a student would create a tree diagram to illustrate all of the possible combinations. A tree diagram makes it possible to quickly show each outcome that results from each previous outcome.

Example 2

What's the Problem?

Ed only eats pizza, oatmeal, and rice. Every day, Ed eats one of three things for breakfast, lunch, and dinner. He only eats 1 item per meal; and once he eats one of these foods, he does not eat it again that day.

How many different combinations of daily meals can Ed have with these 3 foods?

Use a tree diagram to show your work.

Work It Out

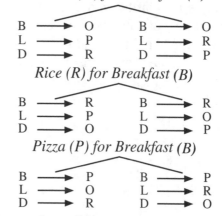

Oatmeal (O) for Breakfast (B)

```
B ──→ O        B ──→ O
L ──→ P        L ──→ R
D ──→ R        D ──→ P
```

Rice (R) for Breakfast (B)

```
B ──→ R        B ──→ R
L ──→ P        L ──→ O
D ──→ O        D ──→ P
```

Pizza (P) for Breakfast (B)

```
B ──→ P        B ──→ P
L ──→ O        L ──→ R
D ──→ R        D ──→ O
```

There are 6 possible outcomes.

How I Solved the Problem

To solve the problem, a student would create a tree diagram to illustrate all of the possible combinations. The student could begin by choosing one of the variables to start with (such as oatmeal for breakfast) and find all combinations using that variable.

Examples of Strategies

Working Backwards

Sometimes a problem seems to be written backwards. It starts with end results and asks you to solve something at the beginning. When this happens, start at the end, with the last piece of information, and work backwards (in reverse order) to find out what happened in the beginning.

Example 1

What's the Problem?

Art, Nick, Paul, and Ty play on the same baseball team. Paul hit 7 more doubles than Nick but 8 fewer than Art. Ty's 44 doubles were twice as many Nick's.

How many doubles did each player hit?

Work It Out

Ty = 44 doubles

Nick = $44 \div 2 = 22$ doubles

Paul = $22 + 7 = 29$ doubles

Art = $29 + 8 = 37$ doubles

How I Solved the Problem

To solve the problem, a student would start with the end result of Ty hitting 44 doubles. From there, the student can figure out Nick's total. This will lead to more answers.

Example 2

What's the Problem?

On Ann's 14th birthday, her uncle said, "I'm thinking of a number between 1 and 50. It's an odd number, and it's divisible by both 3 and 9. This number is more than twice your age! Can you solve this riddle?"

Solve the riddle for Ann.

Work It Out

- The number is less than 50.
- The number is more than twice Ann's age ($14 \times 2 = 28$). That eliminates numbers 1–28.
- The number is divisible by both 3 and 9. That eliminates all but 36 and 45.
- The number is odd. That eliminates 36.
- Only 45 fits the criteria.

How I Solved the Problem

To solve the problem, a student would start with the pieces of information that are given that can eliminate certain answers. From there, each other piece of given information is added, eliminating more and more answers until the only answer that fits all of the criteria remains.

What's the Problem?

Jamie's father offered to give him a dime for every number he could find between 15 and 50 where the digits in the number added to 10. For example, the digits in the number 46 add up to 10.

Which numbers will he find?

_____

How much money did he earn?

_____

What is the pattern of digits that equal 10?

_____

_____

Complete the organized list to show your answers.

> ### REMINDER
> An organized list helps you solve problems by presenting information in a systematic way.
>
> Follow these steps:
> 1. Think of ways to combine the information into a list or chart.
> 2. Decide on a starting point and work in order.
> 3. Keep one item the same while others change.
> 4. Fill in any gaps.
> 5. Record the solution so it is easy to understand.

Work It Out

Numbers Between 15 and 50			Digits That Equal 10
15	22	29	
16	23	30	
17	24		
18	25		
19	26		
20	27		
21	28		

How I Solved the Problem

Warm-Up 2

What's the Problem?

Jessica's mom offered to pay her a quarter for every palindrome she could find between 10 and 100. (A palindrome is a number that reads the same forward as backward, such as 626.)

How much money can Jessica collect from her mother?

_____

How many palindromes could she find between 100 and 200?

_____

Show your work by completing the organized list of palindromes.

REMINDER

An organized list helps you solve problems by presenting information in a systematic way.

Follow these steps:
1. Think of ways to combine the information into a list or chart.
2. Decide on a starting point and work in order.
3. Keep one item the same while others change.
4. Fill in any gaps.
5. Record the solution so it is easy to understand.

Work It Out

Palindromes Between 10 and 100	Palindromes Between 100 and 200
11	
22	

How I Solved the Problem

Warm-Up
3

What's the Problem?

Kori has become very interested in football. She learned that a football team can score 4 different ways.

Touchdown = 6 points   Safety = 2 points

Field Goal = 3 points   Point After Touchdown = 1 point

She wants to answer these questions:

1. **Which final score under 10 is not possible for one team?**

2. **How many different ways can a team score 10 points?**

3. **How many different ways can a team score 6 points?**

4. **What final scores under 10 would not exist if the 2-point safety and 3-point field goal did not exist?**

Create an orginized list to show the answers.

Work It Out

How I Solved the Problem

Warm-Up
4

What's the Problem?

Norma's mom is the school cook. She is making pizza for the entire school and must be careful about wasting supplies. She needs 67 pounds of flour to make the pizzas. The flour comes in 3- and 5-pound bags. She doesn't want to have any extra or unused flour. Norma has to determine how many 3- and 5-pound bags of flour will be just enough for her mother's pizzas.

How many bags of each weight could she use?

_____

Show your work by listing the different possible combinations in the chart below.

REMINDER

An organized list helps you solve problems by presenting information in a systematic way.

Follow these steps:
1. Think of ways to combine the information into a list or chart.
2. Decide on a starting point and work in order.
3. Keep one item the same while others change.
4. Fill in any gaps.
5. Record the solution so it is easy to understand.

Work It Out

3-pound bags	5-pound bags	Total Weight

How I Solved the Problem

What's the Problem?

Mark was a superb athlete. He won a trophy in football as quarterback of the year. He received a trophy as most valuable player in softball. In basketball, he was awarded a trophy as the highest-scoring player. In tennis, his trophy was for winning the city championship. He put the trophies on a shelf in the living room, but he can't decide which order he wants them placed in the row.

How many different ways can he arrange his trophies on the shelf?

REMINDER

An organized list helps you solve problems by presenting information in a systematic way.

Follow these steps:
1. Think of ways to combine the information into a list or chart.
2. Decide on a starting point and work in order.
3. Keep one item the same while others change.
4. Fill in any gaps.
5. Record the solution so it is easy to understand.

Complete the list below to show the arrangements.

S = softball   B = basketball

F = football   T = tennis

Work It Out

1st	2nd	3rd	4th
S	F	B	T
S	F	T	
S			

How I Solved the Problem

What's the Problem?

Laurie likes being in fashion and she doesn't like to repeat her outfits very often. She has 6 different blouses: bright red, ocean blue, hot pink, pure purple, sunny yellow, and deep orange. She has a pair of black shorts, a brown pair of shorts, a white skirt, a striped skirt, and a pair of blue jeans. She can wear any top with any bottoms.

How many different combinations can she make before she has to repeat an outfit?

_____

List the combinations below.

REMINDER

An organized list helps you solve problems by presenting information in a systematic way.

Follow these steps:
1. Think of ways to combine the information into a list or chart.
2. Decide on a starting point and work in order.
3. Keep one item the same while others change.
4. Fill in any gaps.
5. Record the solution so it is easy to understand.

Work It Out

Blouses	Bottoms	Blouses	Bottoms	Blouses	Bottoms

How I Solved the Problem

What's the Problem?

Jeanette has 4 blouses: dark green, bright pink, fire red, and deep blue. She has blue shorts, black jeans, a striped skirt, and a white skirt. She has 2 hats: a French beret and a baseball cap. She always wears a hat.

How many different outfits can she wear without repeating an outfit?

_____

List the combinations below.

Work It Out

Blouses	Bottoms	Hats	Blouses	Bottoms	Hats

How I Solved the Problem

What's the Problem?

Sarah's cheerleading instructor wanted all of her squad to wear the same digits in a 3-digit number on their outfits. She wanted Sarah to assign a 3-digit number to each cheerleader having only the digits 3, 4, and 5 in some order. The digits could be repeated such as 334 or 555. There are 18 cheerleaders on her squad.

Are there enough different numbers to go around?

_____

Are there any extra numbers? If so, how many?

_____

Complete the organized list below to show the possible combinations.

> **REMINDER**
>
> An organized list helps you solve problems by presenting information in a systematic way.
>
> Follow these steps:
> 1. Think of ways to combine the information into a list or chart.
> 2. Decide on a starting point and work in order.
> 3. Keep one item the same while others change.
> 4. Fill in any gaps.
> 5. Record the solution so it is easy to understand.

Work It Out

333

334

335

How I Solved the Problem

Warm-Up 9

What's the Problem?

Brian is traveling in a trailer across the United States with his grandparents. The trip is 3,375 miles long. The first day, they traveled 50 miles. Each day after that, they traveled 25 miles farther than the day before.

How many miles did they travel each day?

How many days did they take to go across country?

_____

Create an organized list below to show your answers.

> **REMINDER**
>
> An organized list helps you solve problems by presenting information in a systematic way.
>
> Follow these steps:
> 1. Think of ways to combine the information into a list or chart.
> 2. Decide on a starting point and work in order.
> 3. Keep one item the same while others change.
> 4. Fill in any gaps.
> 5. Record the solution so it is easy to understand.

Work It Out

Day	Miles Traveled	Running Total	Day	Miles Traveled	Running Total

How I Solved the Problem

What's the Problem?

Kristin and Christopher were playing a board game. They used a spinner with 4 spaces labeled 1, 2, 3, and 4. Each player was allowed 3 consecutive spins. They could move pieces on a board game only if the total of the 3 spins equaled 5.

How many possible combinations could they spin?

_____

How many combinations equaling 5 could they spin?

_____

Create an organized list below to show the possible combinations.

REMINDER

An organized list helps you solve problems by presenting information in a systematic way.

Follow these steps:
1. Think of ways to combine the information into a list or chart.
2. Decide on a starting point and work in order.
3. Keep one item the same while others change.
4. Fill in any gaps.
5. Record the solution so it is easy to understand.

Work It Out

How I Solved the Problem

What's the Problem?

Mariah played a game called Brainbusters with her parents. They paid her in real money. She got a quarter for every answer she got right without needing any help. She got a nickel for every right answer with help. She was given a half dollar for every answer her parents missed. They played 20 rounds with 1 question per round. After not answering any questions incorrectly, Mariah won $4.35 at the end of the game.

How many quarters, nickels, and half dollars did she receive?

_____

Use the chart below to solve the problem.

REMINDER

Guessing and checking helps you find reasonable guesses to solve a problem. For each guess, look at the important information presented in the problem. Check the guess against the information. Base the next guess on the previous result to see if your choices were too large or too small. (Recording your guesses and results in a chart or table also helps.) Repeat the steps until the problem is solved.

Work It Out

Quarters	Nickels	Half Dollars	Total

How I Solved the Problem

Warm-Up 12

What's the Problem?

Mark bought 3 items on sale at Al's Sporting Goods. During that sale, the store was not charging sales tax for any items purchased. He gave the clerk $50 and received 5 cents in change.

What items did Mark buy?

_____

_____

_____

Use the space below to solve the problem.

Al's Sporting Goods Sale	
Baseball glove	$29.50
Football	$15.75
Cleats	$35.75
Bat	$12.95
Catcher's mask	$19.75
Sunglasses	$7. 50

REMINDER

Guessing and checking helps you find reasonable guesses to solve a problem. For each guess, look at the important information presented in the problem. Check the guess against the information. Base the next guess on the previous result to see if your choices were too large or too small. (Recording your guesses and results in a chart or table also helps.) Repeat the steps until the problem is solved.

Work It Out

How I Solved the Problem

What's the Problem?

Jasmine went to the Ladies Sports Emporium. The store was not charging sales tax on items that had a blue dot marked on the tag. She bought 4 of the blue-dot items. Jasmine gave the clerk $120.00 and received $11.55 in change.

What 4 items did she buy?

_____

_____

_____

_____

Use the space below to solve the problem.

Sports Emporium Sale	
Juniors' jacket	$19.95
Exercise DVDs	$49.50
Stretch socks	$11.25
Warm-up sweats	$13.50
Hair scarves (3)	$15.25
Running shoes	$59.75

REMINDER

Guessing and checking helps you find reasonable guesses to solve a problem. For each guess, look at the important information presented in the problem. Check the guess against the information. Base the next guess on the previous result to see if your choices were too large or too small. (Recording your guesses and results in a chart or table also helps.) Repeat the steps until the problem is solved.

Work It Out

How I Solved the Problem

What's the Problem?

Juan Carlos counted the money in his piggy bank. He has $1.48 in change. He has 19 coins. He does not have any dollar or half dollar coins.

How many of each coin does he have?

_____

_____

Use the chart below to solve the problem. Circle the correct answer

Work It Out

Pennies	Nickels	Dimes	Quarters	Total

How I Solved the Problem

Warm-Up 15

What's the Problem?

Jade picked ripe peaches for her elderly neighbor. In a 7-day period, she collected 182 peaches. Each day she picked 6 more peaches than the day before.

How many peaches did she pick each day?

_____

Use the space below to solve the problem. Circle the correct answer.

Work It Out

How I Solved the Problem

What's the Problem?

Four brothers, Lenny, Lyndon, Lionel, and Larry, stood on a scale and found that together they weighed 600 pounds. Lenny weighs exactly twice as much as Larry and half as much as Lyndon. Lionel weighs the same as his twin brother, Larry.

How much does each boy weigh?

_____

_____

Use the space below to solve the problem. Circle the correct answer.

REMINDER

Guessing and checking helps you find reasonable guesses to solve a problem. For each guess, look at the important information presented in the problem. Check the guess against the information. Base the next guess on the previous result to see if your choices were too large or too small. (Recording your guesses and results in a chart or table also helps.) Repeat the steps until the problem is solved.

Work It Out

How I Solved the Problem

What's the Problem?

Valerie spent $41.75 on 11 books at the school book fair. She only bought books with 2 prices. Her gift books for her younger sister cost $2.95 each. Her fifth-grade novels cost $4.50 each. All book prices already included sales tax.

How many books of each type did Valerie buy?

_____

Use the space below to solve the problem. Circle the correct answer.

REMINDER

Guessing and checking helps you find reasonable guesses to solve a problem. For each guess, look at the important information presented in the problem. Check the guess against the information. Base the next guess on the previous result to see if your choices were too large or too small. (Recording your guesses and results in a chart or table also helps.) Repeat the steps until the problem is solved.

Work It Out

.

How I Solved the Problem

Warm-Up 18

What's the Problem?

Keith spent $79.30 in a sporting goods shop during the ski season in Vermont. He bought some beanies to keep his head warm at $7.95 each. He also bought gloves for his hands at $12.15 per pair, and face masks to protect his nose and face at $9.50 each.

How many face masks, beanies, and pairs of gloves did he buy?

_____

Use the space below to solve the problem. Circle the correct answer.

REMINDER

Guessing and checking helps you find reasonable guesses to solve a problem. For each guess, look at the important information presented in the problem. Check the guess against the information. Base the next guess on the previous result to see if your choices were too large or too small. (Recording your guesses and results in a chart or table also helps.) Repeat the steps until the problem is solved.

Work It Out

How I Solved the Problem

What's the Problem?

Clyde was the best basketball player on his team in the local league. In one game he scored 44 points on 21 shots, including 3 one-point foul shots.

How many 2-point field goals and how many 3-point field goals did he make?

_____

Use the chart below to solve the problem. Circle the correct answer.

REMINDER

Guessing and checking helps you find reasonable guesses to solve a problem. For each guess, look at the important information presented in the problem. Check the guess against the information. Base the next guess on the previous result to see if your choices were too large or too small. (Recording your guesses and results in a chart or table also helps.) Repeat the steps until the problem is solved.

Work It Out

1-point	2-point	3-point	Total
3			
3			
3			
3			
3			
3			

How I Solved the Problem

What's the Problem?

Pam and John were playing a card game where you received 10 points for every face card and 4 points for every number card left in your opponent's hand. John earned 60 points from the 9 cards in Pam's hand.

How many were face cards and how many were number cards?

_____

Use the space below to solve the problem. Circle the correct answer.

REMINDER

Guessing and checking helps you find reasonable guesses to solve a problem. For each guess, look at the important information presented in the problem. Check the guess against the information. Base the next guess on the previous result to see if your choices were too large or too small. (Recording your guesses and results in a chart or table also helps.) Repeat the steps until the problem is solved.

Work It Out

How I Solved the Problem

Warm-Up
21

What's the Problem?

Mario's father let him ride a busy metro train for 2 hours one morning for a school project. He observed that 1 passenger boarded the train at the first stop. Four passengers got on at the second stop, 10 passengers got aboard at the third stop, and 22 boarded at the fourth stop.

If this pattern continued, how many passengers boarded at the 9th stop?

_____

What pattern of passenger boarding did Mario find?

_____

How many passengers boarded the train during the 9 stops?

_____

Create a list in the space below and look for a pattern to solve the problem.

> ## REMINDER
>
> Looking for patterns makes it easier to predict what comes next. In a problem, study any number patterns to see how the numbers change from one number to the next. For example, to find the rule for the pattern, 2, 7, 22, 67, study how 2 and 7, 7 and 22 are related, etc. You will see that each number is 3 times the number before it plus 1, or (n x 3) + 1.

Work It Out

How I Solved the Problem

What's the Problem?

After school, Maria rode the metro train to her grandmother's home for a visit. She counted 194 passengers when she got on, including herself, and 59 more passengers boarded the train. On the train's first stop, 9 people got off the train. At the second stop, 17 left the train. On the third stop, 33 left the train.

If no other people boarded the train and the pattern of people leaving continued, how many stops did the train make in order for all passengers to get off?

_____

How many people left at the last stop?

_____

Create a list in the space below and look for a pattern to solve the problem.

Work It Out

How I Solved the Problem

What's the Problem?

Jill is getting in shape for her swim team. The first day she swam 1 lap in the pool. The second day she swam 2 laps. On the third day she swam 4 laps, and she swam 7 laps on the fourth day.

If this pattern continued, how many laps did she swim on the 8th day?

_____

What is the pattern?

_____

Create a list in the space below and look for a pattern to solve the problem.

REMINDER

Looking for patterns makes it easier to predict what comes next. In a problem, study any number patterns to see how the numbers change from one number to the next. For example, to find the rule for the pattern, 2, 7, 22, 67, study how 2 and 7, 7 and 22 are related, etc. You will see that each number is 3 times the number before it plus 1, or $(n \times 3) + 1$.

Work It Out

How I Solved the Problem

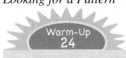

What's the Problem?

Caleb's eccentric uncle gives out silver dollars to his nieces and nephews according to their ages. He gave 1 silver dollar to the youngest baby and 1 silver dollar to the second youngest baby. He passed out 2 silver dollars to the next youngest and 3 silver dollars to the next child. The following child got 5 silver dollars, and the next child got 8 dollars.

If this pattern continued, how many dollars did the seventh, eighth, and ninth children get?

_____

Caleb was tenth. How many silver dollars did he get?

_____

Create a list in the space below and look for a pattern to solve the problem.

REMINDER

Looking for patterns makes it easier to predict what comes next. In a problem, study any number patterns to see how the numbers change from one number to the next. For example, to find the rule for the pattern, 2, 7, 22, 67, study how 2 and 7, 7 and 22 are related, etc. You will see that each number is 3 times the number before it plus 1, or (n x 3) + 1.

Work It Out

How I Solved the Problem

What's the Problem?

Raymond was raising chickens on his farm. The first week, 2 chicks hatched. The second week, 7 chicks hatched. The third week, 17 chicks hatched. 317 chicks hatched the seventh week.

If this pattern continued, how many chicks hatched in the fourth, fifth, and sixth weeks?

_____

What is the pattern?

_____

Create a list in the space below and look for a pattern to solve the problem.

REMINDER

Looking for patterns makes it easier to predict what comes next. In a problem, study any number patterns to see how the numbers change from one number to the next. For example, to find the rule for the pattern, 2, 7, 22, 67, study how 2 and 7, 7 and 22 are related, etc. You will see that each number is 3 times the number before it plus 1, or (n x 3) + 1.

Work It Out

How I Solved the Problem

Warm-Up
26

What's the Problem?

Marty agreed to pick all of the lemons off his neighbor's tall lemon tree. Because it was a long, hard job, his neighbor offered to pay him 1 cent for the first lemon, 3 cents for the second lemon, 6 cents for the third lemon, and 10 cents for the fourth lemon.

Based on this pattern, how much will Marty earn for the 10th lemon?

_____

If the tree has 15 lemons, how much will he earn for that 15th lemon?

_____

Create a list in the space below and look for a pattern to solve the problem.

> ### REMINDER
>
> Looking for patterns makes it easier to predict what comes next. In a problem, study any number patterns to see how the numbers change from one number to the next. For example, to find the rule for the pattern, 2, 7, 22, 67, study how 2 and 7, 7 and 22 are related, etc. You will see that each number is 3 times the number before it plus 1, or (n x 3) + 1.

Work It Out

How I Solved the Problem

What's the Problem?

Stephanie is reading a novel for her book report project. She found that the first 4 chapters of her novel began on pages 1, 4, 9, and 16.

Following this pattern, on what pages will the next 4 chapters begin?

_____

What is the pattern?

_____

Create a list in the space below and look for a pattern to solve the problem.

> ## REMINDER
>
> Looking for patterns makes it easier to predict what comes next. In a problem, study any number patterns to see how the numbers change from one number to the next. For example, to find the rule for the pattern, 2, 7, 22, 67, study how 2 and 7, 7 and 22 are related, etc. You will see that each number is 3 times the number before it plus 1, or $(n \times 3) + 1$.

Work It Out

How I Solved the Problem

What's the Problem?

James found these numbers listed in a book of magic spells with this message: "Find the missing numbers. Turn to the page named by the middle term. Find a spell to help you make your baby brother fall asleep."

(17, 26, 37, _____, _____, _____, 101, 122, 145)

What is the page number with the spell?

_____

What is the pattern?

_____

Use the space below to solve the problem.

> **REMINDER**
>
> Looking for patterns makes it easier to predict what comes next. In a problem, study any number patterns to see how the numbers change from one number to the next. For example, to find the rule for the pattern, 2, 7, 22, 67, study how 2 and 7, 7 and 22 are related, etc. You will see that each number is 3 times the number before it plus 1, or (n x 3) + 1.

Work It Out

How I Solved the Problem

What's the Problem?

Jerry visited a medical lab with his school science club. The company was incubating fruit flies to use for medical tests. The first hour, there were only 2 fruit flies. There were 4 in the second hour and 8 in the third hour.

At this rate, how many flies will incubate at the 13th hour?

_____

What is the pattern?

_____

Create a list in the space below and look for a pattern to solve the problem.

REMINDER

Looking for patterns makes it easier to predict what comes next. In a problem, study any number patterns to see how the numbers change from one number to the next. For example, to find the rule for the pattern, 2, 7, 22, 67, study how 2 and 7, 7 and 22 are related, etc. You will see that each number is 3 times the number before it plus 1, or $(n \times 3) + 1$.

Work It Out

How I Solved the Problem

What's the Problem?

Eric and his school ecology club did their community service by collecting trash at the beach. In their first week, they collected 80 bags of trash. They filled only 40 bags the second week and 20 bags the third week.

Following this pattern, how many bags will they collect each week over the next 4 weeks?

_____

What is the pattern?

_____

Create a list in the space below and look for a pattern to solve the problem.

> ## REMINDER
>
> Looking for patterns makes it easier to predict what comes next. In a problem, study any number patterns to see how the numbers change from one number to the next. For example, to find the rule for the pattern, 2, 7, 22, 67, study how 2 and 7, 7 and 22 are related, etc. You will see that each number is 3 times the number before it plus 1, or (n x 3) + 1.

Work It Out

How I Solved the Problem

What's the Problem?

Stephanie and Erica can't decide which ice cream treat to buy. They have a choice between chocolate or strawberry ice cream, a cup or a cone, and a topping of chocolate syrup or whipped cream.

How many possible ice cream combinations do they have to choose from?

_____

Make tree diagrams in the space below to illustrate the possible outcomes.

REMINDER

Create a tree diagram to show how the different items in a problem are connected. This strategy is helpful for solving problems where you need to find all possible combinations of the items. Begin by organizing a list of the items. Link each item into a tree diagram until all possible combinations are shown. Use the results to help solve the problem.

Work It Out

How I Solved the Problem

What's the Problem?

Michael is flipping 2 coins, a quarter and a dime, 2 separate times each.

How many different possible outcomes for each coin can result from flipping these coins twice?

_____

Use tree diagrams to show all the possible outcomes. Draw them in the space below.

REMINDER

Create a tree diagram to show how the different items in a problem are connected. This strategy is helpful for solving problems where you need to find all possible combinations of the items. Begin by organizing a list of the items. Link each item into a tree diagram until all possible combinations are shown. Use the results to help solve the problem.

Work It Out

How I Solved the Problem

Warm-Up 33

What's the Problem?

Sonia was studying the family car, which had 4 letters on the license plate: LOVE. She wondered how many different ways those 4 letters could be arranged.

How many different possible arrangements can there be?

_____

Use tree diagrams to determine all of the possible arrangements. Draw them in the space below.

Work It Out

How I Solved the Problem

What's the Problem?

Rebecca, Jonathan, and Clinton are triplets, and they have to share everything. After receiving a tandem (2 seat) bicycle for their birthday, they took turns riding it around the block.

How many different arrangements can they have in riding the tandem bicycle?

_____

Use tree diagrams to illustrate the different seating arrangements. Draw them in the space below.

> ## REMINDER
>
> Create a tree diagram to show how the different items in a problem are connected. This strategy is helpful for solving problems where you need to find all possible combinations of the items. Begin by organizing a list of the items. Link each item into a tree diagram until all possible combinations are shown. Use the results to help solve the problem.

Work It Out

How I Solved the Problem

What's the Problem?

Miriam, Elena, Christina, and Sarah were the final 4 in their school field day 50-yard dash. All of them are very fast runners.

How many possible ways could the race end?

_____

Create tree diagrams in the space below to show all of the possible arrangements in which they could finish. One diagram is started for you.

Work It Out

1st	2nd	3rd	4th

```
              C — S
      E <
              S — C

M <   C

      S
```

How I Solved the Problem

Warm-Up
36

What's the Problem?

Catherine is playing a game that has a spinner with 3 sections labeled 1, 2, and 3. She wanted to know what the probability is for spinning the spinner 3 times in a row and getting a 3 each time.

How many possible outcomes are there when spinning 3 times?

_____

What is the probability of landing on a 3 each time?

_____

Make tree diagrams in the space below to illustrate all of the possible results.

REMINDER

Create a tree diagram to show how the different items in a problem are connected. This strategy is helpful for solving problems where you need to find all possible combinations of the items. Begin by organizing a list of the items. Link each item into a tree diagram until all possible combinations are shown. Use the results to help solve the problem.

Work It Out

How I Solved the Problem

What's the Problem?

Michael was bored while in the waiting room at his doctor's office. He decided to flip 2 quarters 3 different times.

How many different possible outcomes can result from flipping these coins?

_____

Use a tree diagram to show the possible outcomes. Draw it in the space below.

REMINDER

Create a tree diagram to show how the different items in a problem are connected. This strategy is helpful for solving problems where you need to find all possible combinations of the items. Begin by organizing a list of the items. Link each item into a tree diagram until all possible combinations are shown. Use the results to help solve the problem.

Work It Out

How I Solved the Problem

Warm-Up 38

What's the Problem?

Christian and Matthew went to the Pronto Pizza Parlor. They could choose a small, medium, or large pizza. They had a choice between regular, thick, or thin dough. They could order cheese, pepperoni, or vegetable toppings.

How many different kinds of pizza could they order?

_____

Create tree diagrams in the space below to illustrate all of the possible outcomes.

REMINDER

Create a tree diagram to show how the different items in a problem are connected. This strategy is helpful for solving problems where you need to find all possible combinations of the items. Begin by organizing a list of the items. Link each item into a tree diagram until all possible combinations are shown. Use the results to help solve the problem.

Work It Out

How I Solved the Problem

What's the Problem?

Eric and Steven were playing a game with a tetrahedral die (a die with 4 faces) with the numbers 1 to 4 on the die. Eric rolled the die 3 times.

How many possible outcomes of numbers he could roll?

_____

Use tree diagrams to illustrate all of the possible outcomes. Draw them in the space below.

REMINDER

Create a tree diagram to show how the different items in a problem are connected. This strategy is helpful for solving problems where you need to find all possible combinations of the items. Begin by organizing a list of the items. Link each item into a tree diagram until all possible combinations are shown. Use the results to help solve the problem.

Work It Out

How I Solved the Problem

What's the Problem?

Alexis received 3 certificates in Reading, Creative Writing, and Drama. She wanted to arrange the framed certificates on the wall in the family living room. She couldn't decide exactly which certificate she wanted first, second, and third.

How many different ways can she arrange the certificates?

_____

Make tree diagrams in the space below to show all of the possible arrangements.

REMINDER

Create a tree diagram to show how the different items in a problem are connected. This strategy is helpful for solving problems where you need to find all possible combinations of the items. Begin by organizing a list of the items. Link each item into a tree diagram until all possible combinations are shown. Use the results to help solve the problem.

Work It Out

How I Solved the Problem

What's the Problem?

Grandpa paid his grandchildren 13 cents for each earthworm they collected before he went fishing. Jill collected 16 more fishing worms than Reggie. Jonathan collected 17 less than Reggie. Anne collected 15 worms more than Jill. Joseph collected 11 more worms than Jonathan, who collected 18 worms.

How many worms did each child collect?

_____

_____

How much money did Grandpa pay each child?

_____

_____

Use the space below to solve the problem.

REMINDER

Sometimes a problem seems to be written backwards. It starts with end results and asks you to solve something at the beginning. When this happens, start at the end, with the last piece of information, and work backwards (in reverse order) to find out what happened in the beginning.

Work It Out

How I Solved the Problem

What's the Problem?

Jamie gathered a large basket of vegetables from the family garden. There are 3 times as many potatoes as turnips. There are twice as many ears of corn as potatoes. Eleven of the vegetables are either tomatoes or beets. There are 5 beets. There are 4 times as many potatoes as tomatoes.

How many vegetables of each kind did Jamie gather?

_____

_____

Use the space below to solve the problem.

> ### REMINDER
> Sometimes a problem seems to be written backwards. It starts with end results and asks you to solve something at the beginning. When this happens, start at the end, with the last piece of information, and work backwards (in reverse order) to find out what happened in the beginning.

Work It Out

How I Solved the Problem

Warm-Up
43

What's the Problem?

Mike, Joe, Jimmy, Art, and Steve each stood on a platform of the playground apparatus and threw a Super Duper Bouncing Ball at the blacktop. They counted the bounces. Joe's ball bounced 6 more times than Mike's ball. Art's ball bounced 4 more times than Joe's. Jimmy's ball bounced 8 more times than Joe's. Steve's ball bounced 16 times, which was 1 less bounce than Jimmy's ball.

How many times did each boy's ball bounce?

_____

_____

Use the space below to solve the problem.

> ### REMINDER
> Sometimes a problem seems to be written backwards. It starts with end results and asks you to solve something at the beginning. When this happens, start at the end, with the last piece of information, and work backwards (in reverse order) to find out what happened in the beginning.

Work It Out

How I Solved the Problem

What's the Problem?

Ricky, Roman, Roger, and Roland went fishing with their grandfather. A big fish caught by Roman was twice as big as Ricky's. Ricky's was twice as large as Roland's. Roger's fish was 32 ounces. It was half the size of their grandfather's. Grandfather's was 2 times as large as Roman's.

How much did each person's fish weigh?

_____

_____

Use the space below to solve the problem.

REMINDER

Sometimes a problem seems to be written backwards. It starts with end results and asks you to solve something at the beginning. When this happens, start at the end, with the last piece of information, and work backwards (in reverse order) to find out what happened in the beginning.

Work It Out

How I Solved the Problem

Warm-Up
45

What's the Problem?

Shane's friends held a marble tournament. Shane had 6 more marbles than Monica. Monica and Minnie had 17 marbles between them. Joey had 8 fewer marbles than Shane. Minnie had 5 marbles. Erica had 1 more marble than Shane.

How many marbles did each friend have?

_____

_____

Who had the most marbles?

_____

Use the space below to solve the problem.

> **REMINDER**
>
> Sometimes a problem seems to be written backwards. It starts with end results and asks you to solve something at the beginning. When this happens, start at the end, with the last piece of information, and work backwards (in reverse order) to find out what happened in the beginning.

Work It Out

How I Solved the Problem

What's the Problem?

Shirlene helps her grandmother raise goldfish in her garden pond. In 1 week, her grandmother gave 10 fish to each of 4 friends who came to visit. During that week, Shirlene counted 37 baby fish that hatched and 7 adult fish that died. At the end of the week, they had 88 fish in the pond.

How many fish did they have at the beginning of the week?

_____

Use the space below to solve the problem.

> **REMINDER**
>
> Sometimes a problem seems to be written backwards. It starts with end results and asks you to solve something at the beginning. When this happens, start at the end, with the last piece of information, and work backwards (in reverse order) to find out what happened in the beginning.

Work It Out

How I Solved the Problem

What's the Problem?

Yo-yos are the latest fad at Amy's after-school program. She can keep her yo-yo in motion twice as long as Alana, but only half as long as Allison. Anthony can yo-yo twice as long as Allison, but only half as long as Ashton. Arto can yo-yo for 4 minutes, which is half as long as Alana.

How long can each student keep his or her yo-yo in motion?

_____

_____

_____

Use the space below to solve the problem.

REMINDER

Sometimes a problem seems to be written backwards. It starts with end results and asks you to solve something at the beginning. When this happens, start at the end, with the last piece of information, and work backwards (in reverse order) to find out what happened in the beginning.

Work It Out

How I Solved the Problem

Warm-Up
48

What's the Problem?

Albert posed this puzzle to his friends in the fifth-grade science club. "My favorite planet is farther from Earth than Earth is from the sun. My favorite planet is farther from the dwarf planet Pluto than it is from Earth. It is farther from the sun than the combined distances of Jupiter and Saturn from the sun."

What is Albert's favorite planet?

_____

Use the space below to solve the problem.

Planet	Distance from the Sun (million miles)
Mercury	36
Venus	67
Earth	92
Mars	142
Jupiter	483
Saturn	887
Uranus	1,783
Neptune	2,794
Pluto (dwarf)	3,660

REMINDER

Sometimes a problem seems to be written backwards. It starts with end results and asks you to solve something at the beginning. When this happens, start at the end, with the last piece of information, and work backwards (in reverse order) to find out what happened in the beginning.

Work It Out

How I Solved the Problem

What's the Problem?

Jill keeps her pet alligator lizard in a large terrarium. The length of the terrarium is 3 times the width. The height is one-half of the length. The width is twice the length of the lizard. The lizard is 10 inches long from tip to tail.

What is the volume of the terrarium?

_____

Use the space below to solve the problem.

REMINDER

Sometimes a problem seems to be written backwards. It starts with end results and asks you to solve something at the beginning. When this happens, start at the end, with the last piece of information, and work backwards (in reverse order) to find out what happened in the beginning.

Work It Out

How I Solved the Problem

What's the Problem?

Katy is in the fifth grade. She is 10 years old. Her sister, Katrina, is 3 times as old as Caroline. Carmen is 3 years older than Katrina and 5 years younger than Kristin. Caroline is half as old as Katy.

How old is each girl?

_____

_____

_____

Use the space below to solve the problem.

Work It Out

How I Solved the Problem

What's the Problem?

Work It Out

Jeremiah's father wanted to test Jeremiah's math skills. He posed these 3 questions to him. He leveled the first question as easy, the second question as hard, and the third as very hard.

1. **Which numbers from 2 to 9 will divide evenly into 72?**

   _____

2. **Which numbers from 2 to 9 will divide evenly into 331?**

   _____

3. **Which numbers from 2 to 9 will divide evenly into 441?**

   _____

Compute the answers.

• •

What's the Problem?

Work It Out

Jeremiah posed these 3 questions for his father. He leveled the first question as easy, the second question as hard, and the third question as very hard.

1. **Which numbers from 2 to 9 will divide evenly into 91?**

   _____

2. **Which numbers from 2 to 9 will divide evenly into 337?**

   _____

3. **Which numbers from 2 to 9 will divide evenly into 423?**

   _____

Compute the answers.

Warm-Up 53

What's the Problem?

Work It Out

Freddy found a fast method for dividing large numbers. He realized that he could divide 200 into 1,000 in a few seconds and that the answer is 5. He demonstrated his method for his class this way:

$$\frac{1,0\cancel{0}\cancel{0}}{2\cancel{0}\cancel{0}}$$

Freddy drew a line through the last 2 zeros of each number and then divided 2 into 10, which is 5. He pointed out that 5 times 200 equals 1,000 as proof of his method.

Use Freddy's method to solve these problems:

1. 5000 ÷ 50 = _____

2. 40,000 ÷ 8,000 = _____

3. 90,000 ÷ 3,000 = _____

4. 63,000 ÷ 900 = _____

5. 64,000 ÷ 8,000 = _____

6. 84,000 ÷ 12,000 = _____

• •

Warm-Up 54

What's the Problem?

Work It Out

Freddy was so pleased with his discovery that he demonstrated how he could divide millions in a few seconds. He divided 81,000,000 by 9,000,000.

$$\frac{81,\cancel{0}\cancel{0}\cancel{0},\cancel{0}\cancel{0}\cancel{0}}{9,\cancel{0}\cancel{0}\cancel{0},\cancel{0}\cancel{0}\cancel{0}} = 9$$

Freddy pointed out that the proof was that 9 times 9,000,000 equaled 81,000,000.

Use Freddy's method to divide these millions:

1. 72,000,000 ÷ 8,000,000 = _____

2. 36,000,000 ÷ 4,000,000 = _____

3. 49,000,000 ÷ 7,000,000 = _____

4. 100,000,000 ÷ 20,000,000 = _____

5. 66,000,000 ÷ 33,000 = _____

6. 25,000,000 ÷ 5,000 = _____

What's the Problem?

Work It Out

Briana sold 20 boxes of chocolate cream cookies for the school fundraiser at $8.39 each. She sold 12 boxes of vanilla cream cookies for $7.69 each.

How much money did she collect altogether for the fundraiser?

_____

What's the Problem?

Work It Out

Briana's school sold $4,139 worth of cookies during the fundraiser. The school receives 30% of the money raised from the cookie fundraiser.

How much money did the school receive?

_____

What's the Problem?   Work It Out

Serena and Sarah helped their mother make fudge for their classroom parties in different classes. Serena's class received $2\frac{1}{2}$ pounds for 25 children. Sarah's class received $3\frac{1}{2}$ pounds for 35 children.

1. How much fudge did they make altogether?

_____

2. How much fudge did each child get in Serena's class?

_____

3. How much fudge did each child get in Sarah's class?

_____

What's the Problem?   Work It Out

Sarah and Serena are twins and often receive gifts that they have to share. Their grandmother gave them $7\frac{1}{2}$ yards of fabric to make nightgowns and $1\frac{1}{4}$ yards of ribbon for their hair. They split the fabric and ribbon evenly between them.

1. How much fabric did each twin receive?

_____

2. How much ribbon did each girl have?

_____

Warm-Up 59

What's the Problem?

Work It Out

Nathan and Natalie picked all the apples off of the 18 apple trees in their apple grove. The local grocery store paid them $0.06 each for every good apple. A neighbor who made homemade cider gave them $0.03 for every apple that was dented, small, or rejected by the grocery store. They sold 540 apples to the grocery store and 270 apples to the cider maker.

1. How much were they paid by the grocery store?

_____

2. How much were they paid by the cider maker?

_____

3. How much were they paid altogether?

_____

4. What was the average number of apples they picked off each tree?

_____

Warm-Up 60

Work It Out

1. Nathan and Natalie split the money evenly. How much money did each child receive?

_____

2. Nathan wanted to use his money to buy a baseball glove that cost $43.79. Did he have enough money?

_____

3. How much did he have left over or how much money did he need?

_____

4. Natalie wanted a pair of jeans that cost $57.99. How much more money did Natalie need?

_____

What's the Problem?

Work It Out

During a science lesson on the human heart, students recorded their heartbeats for 1 minute. Brian's pulse rate or heartbeat was 88. Agnes had an 86. Jennifer's pulse rate was 96. Adrian's was 79. Jerome had a 90, and Alicia's was 95.

1. **What was the average pulse rate of all 6 students?**

   _____

2. **What was the average pulse rate of the 3 boys?**

   _____

3. **What was the average pulse rate of the 3 girls?**

   _____

What's the Problem?

Work It Out

1. **The entire class of 32 students totaled their heartbeats in 1 minute. It was 2,899 heartbeats. What was the average heartbeat for the class?**

   _____

2. **Sixteen students recorded the pulse rates of their mothers. The total for the 16 mothers was 1,248 heartbeats. What was the average mother's pulse rate?**

   _____

3. **Sixteen students recorded the pulse rates of their fathers. The total for the 16 fathers was 1,120 heartbeats. What was the average father's pulse rate?**

   _____

What's the Problem?

Work It Out

Corina intends to be a doctor when she grows up. She is especially interested in human digestion. Corina learned that the acid in the stomach is so powerful and corrosive that the stomach has to produce a new lining every 3 days. Stomach acid is so strong it could even dissolve small bones and bits of metal.

1. **About how many stomach linings must a human grow in 1 year?**

   _____

2. **About how many stomach linings has a 79-year-old person produced?**

   _____

3. **About how many stomach linings have you produced?**

   _____

What's the Problem?

Work It Out

Corina read that the stomach lining sheds and makes about 500,000 cells every minute.

1. **About how many cells does the stomach make in 1 hour?**

   _____

2. **About how many cells does the stomach make in 1 day?**

   _____

3. **About how many cells does the stomach make in 1 second?**

   _____

What's the Problem?

Work It Out

In science class, Brittany learned that the human body is composed of about 62% water, 17% protein, and 15% fat. She knew that she weighed 90 pounds.

1. How much of Brittany's weight is water?

_____

2. How much of her weight is protein?

_____

3. How much of her weight is fat?

_____

4. How much of her weight is not accounted for?

_____

What's the Problem?

Work It Out

Brittany's classmates volunteered their weight. Jeffrey weighed 143 pounds. Teresa weighed 100 pounds. Hazel weighed 68 pounds, and Jonathan weighed 112 pounds.

How many pounds of water, protein, and fat did each classmate have?

_____

_____

_____

_____

_____

_____

_____

What's the Problem?

Work It Out

Kimberly was interested in how many people lived in her country, her state, and her city, but she wanted numbers that were easy to remember and compare.

Her country has 301,621,157 people.

Her state has 36,553,215 people.

Her city has 3,834,340 people.

What is the population of these places rounded to the nearest million?

_____

_____

_____

• •

What's the Problem?

Work It Out

Kimberly listed these states and their populations.

State	Population	State	Population
NY	19,297,729	WV	1,812,035
CA	36,553,215	MT	957,861
HI	1,283,388	NV	2,565,382
TX	23,904,380	MN	5,197,621
MI	10,071,822	OH	11,466,917

NY =

CA =

HI =

TX =

MI =

WV =

MT =

NV =

MN =

OH =

1. **Round each population to the nearest million.**

2. **Which of these states has the largest population?** _____

3. **Which of these states has the lowest population?** _____

4. **How do rounded numbers help make the figures easier to understand and more meaningful?** _____

_____

What's the Problem?

Work It Out

Tim was interested in how long famous people lived. He looked up these famous presidents:

Thomas Jefferson was born April 13, 1743 and died July 4, 1826.

John Adams was born October 30, 1735 and died July 4, 1826.

James Monroe was born April 28, 1758 and died July 4, 1831.

Compute the age of each president when he died. Write the ages next to the names.

(Reminder: The person must live past his birthday in his last year to just subtract the years. For example, Adams will be 1 year less than the subtracted years.)

What's the Problem?

Work It Out

Tim was also interested in famous scientists. He found these dates:

Rachel Carson	1907 – 1964
Marie Curie	1867 – 1934
Alexander Graham Bell	1847 – 1922
Jacques Yves Costeau	1910 – 1997
Thomas Edison	1847 – 1931
Albert Einstein	1879 – 1955

About how old was each of these scientists when he or she died? Write the ages next to the names.

72

Warm-Up 71

What's the Problem?   Work It Out

Julian received $80 in gift money from his family.
He spent 50% of the money on a baseball glove.

1. **How much money did Julian have left?** _____

2. **Julian spent 50% of the remaining money on baseballs. How much money did he have left?**

    _____

3. **Julian spent 50% of the remaining money on baseball cards. How much money did he have left?**

    _____

4. **He spent 50% of the remaining money on a baseball cap. How much money did Julian have left?**

    _____

5. **He spent 50% of the remaining money on sunglasses. How much money did he have left to buy a sticker at the stadium?**

    _____

Warm-Up 72

What's the Problem?   Work It Out

Julian's dad took him to the baseball stadium for his birthday.
He spent $100 at the stadium.

1. **Tickets cost 40% of the money. How much money did tickets cost?** _____

2. **Hot dogs and drinks cost 25% of the money. How much money did hot dogs and drinks cost?**

    _____

3. **Popcorn cost 8% of the money. How much money did Julian's dad spend on popcorn?**

    _____

4. **T-shirts cost 10% of the money and parking cost 7% of the money. How much money did Julian's dad spend on T-shirts? How much money was spent on parking?** _____

5. **How much money was left for Julian to buy dessert?**

    _____

Warm-Up 73

What's the Problem?   **Work It Out**

Jade, Jennifer, Julia, and Justine bought a large pizza together and told the cook to cut it into 24 equal pieces.

Janet ate $\frac{1}{6}$ of the pizza.   Julia ate $\frac{1}{4}$.

Jennifer ate $\frac{1}{3}$ of the pizza.   Justine ate $\frac{1}{8}$.

1. How many pieces did each girl eat?

_____

_____

2. How many pieces were left?

_____

3. What fractional part of the pizza was left?

_____

Warm-Up 74

What's the Problem?   **Work It Out**

On Saturday, Justine's brother ate $\frac{1}{2}$ of a pizza for lunch and $\frac{1}{4}$ of the pizza for dinner.

1. What fractional part of the pizza did he eat altogether?

_____

2. What fractional part of the pizza was left?

_____

Warm-Up 75

What's the Problem?

Work It Out

April measured the amount of square feet on the property where her family lives. The entire lot is 8,000 square feet.

The house takes up 30% of the area.

The garage takes up 20% of the area.

The lawn takes up 25% of the area.

The driveway takes up 10% of the lot.

The flower gardens take up 8% of the lot.

The sidewalk takes up 7% of the lot.

What is the area of each measured part?

_____

_____

_____

● ●

Warm-Up 76

What's the Problem?

Work It Out

1. **Which 3 areas together occupy the same amount of area as the lawn?**

   _____

   _____

2. **Which 2 areas take up $\frac{1}{2}$ of the entire lot?**

   _____

3. **Which 4 areas occupy $\frac{1}{2}$ of the lot together?**

   _____

   _____

   _____

**Warm-Up
77**

What's the Problem?

Work It Out

Jung posed this question to his friend, Phillip: "Which of these numbers has the greatest number of factors?"

(3, 13, 25, 37, 41, 47)

1. **Find the number with the greatest number of factors.**

   _____

2. **Explain why the other numbers have such few factors.**

   _____

   _____

   _____

   _____

**Warm-Up
78**

What's the Problem?

Work It Out

Phillip made a list of the numbers below and challenged Jung to find the number with the greatest number of factors.

(9, 12, 18, 36, 64, 72, 99, 100)

1. **Which of these numbers has the greatest number of factors?**

   _____

2. **Which of these numbers has the fewest factors?**

   _____

What's the Problem?

Work It Out

Natasha and Jonathan ran their own lawn-mowing business in the summer. They charged $17 for large lawns and $9.50 for smaller lawns. During their first month, they mowed 13 large lawns and 23 small lawns.

1. **How much money were they paid altogether?**

   _____

2. **Their expenses for gas and other supplies totaled $61.54. What was their profit after paying their expenses?**

   _____

What's the Problem?

Work It Out

1. **Natasha and Jonathan split the profit evenly. How much did each of them receive?**

   _____

2. **Natasha invested her money in a savings account paying 5% interest per year. How much interest will she earn at the end of 1 year?**

   _____

What's the Problem?   Work It Out

Mariah posed this question to her math partner, Nicholas: "What is the highest number, greater than 12 and less than 50, that has a factor tree where all of its prime numbers are only 2 and 3?"

Make the factor trees and circle your answer.

What's the Problem?   Work It Out

Nicholas posed this question to Mariah: "What is the highest number, greater than 50 and less than 100, that has a factor tree where all of its prime numbers are only 2 and 3?"

Make the factor trees and circle your answer.

What's the Problem?   Work It Out

Matthew's teacher asked the students to find and count all the prime numbers between 1 and 100. He knew that prime numbers have only 2 factors: 1 and the number itself. He also knew that the number 1 was neither prime nor composite.

1. **What is the only even prime number?** _____

2. **List all of the prime numbers between 1 and 100 that you can.**

_____

_____

_____

_____

_____

What's the Problem?   Work It Out

Matthew told his friend that the largest prime number less than 1,000 was 999.

Do you think he was right? Why or why not?

_____

_____

_____

_____

_____

_____

_____

What's the Problem?

Work It Out

Doreen received these grades on her last 5 math tests: 88, 87, 95, 78, and 100. She was hoping to have an average of 90 or better.

1. **Did Doreen meet her goal if her average was rounded to the nearest whole number?**

   _____

2. **Compute her average in her spelling tests: 100, 97, 88, 93, 100, 66, and 99. Round it to the nearest whole number.**

   _____

- -

What's the Problem?

Work It Out

Doreen was looking at the famous symbol π, which is a decimal that does not terminate or end. It has been carried out to billions of places on super computers. She saw the listed value as 3.14159, which is a little larger than 3. She knew that 3.14159 rounded to the nearest ten thousandth is 3.1416

1. **Round 3.1416 to the nearest thousandth.**

   _____

2. **Round 3.1416 to the nearest hundredth.**

   _____

3. **Round 3.1416 to the nearest tenth.**

   _____

4. **Round 3.1416 to the nearest whole number.**

   _____

Warm-Up 87

What's the Problem?

Work It Out

Their teacher challenged 4 members of the fifth-grade math club, Kevin, Julian, Alexandra, and Jolene, to a contest. The winner would be the first person who could mentally add the following series of decimals to the nearest whole number. The closest answer would win.

1. **Mentally add these numbers. Try to do it in less than a minute.**

   _____

2. **Check your answer by adding the decimals exactly.**

   _____

```
   3.8
   4.5
   6.7
   2.4
   8.9
   5.6
 + 4.3
```

- -

Warm-Up 88

What's the Problem?

Work It Out

Kevin posed this problem for his teacher: Could he add this column of money to the nearest dollar in 30 seconds or less?

1. **Mentally add these numbers. Try to do it in less than a minute.**

   _____

2. **Check your answer by adding the money exactly.**

   _____

```
   $4.98
   $5.99
   $3.13
   $8.48
   $6.72
   $9.99
 + $5.77
```

Warm-Up 89

What's the Problem?

Work It Out

Yvonne bought 5 blouses for $17.95 each and 4 pairs of jeans for $29.89 each. She also purchased a pair of tennis shoes for $59.19 and a jacket for $69.99.

1. **Without tax, what was the total cost of her purchase?**

   _____

2. **Yvonne got a 20% discount because her purchase was over $200. How much was the discount?**

   _____

3. **What was the subtotal after the discount?**

   _____

What's the Problem?

Work It Out

There is a 9% sales tax in Yvonne's city.

1. **How much was the sales tax on her purchase?**

   _____

2. **What was the final cost of Yvonne's purchase including tax?**

   _____

3. **Yvonne paid with 3 one hundred dollar bills. How much change did she receive?**

   _____

Warm-Up 91

What's the Problem?

Work It Out

Sheila drew this equilateral triangle with a perimeter of 3 centimeters. She used it to draw the shapes in the chart.

1. **What is the perimeter of each of the geometric figures shown?**

2. **How many equilateral triangles make up each figure?**

Complete the chart.

Geometric Figure		Perimeter	# of Equilateral Triangles
equilateral triangle			
rhombus			
regular trapezoid			
parallelogram			

Warm-Up 92

What's the Problem?

Work It Out

Sheila wanted to know how many isosceles right triangles she could create inside the shapes below.

1. **How can she create 2, 4, and 8 isosceles right triangles inside the squares?**

2. **How can she create 4 isosceles right triangles inside the rectangle?**

Show your answers in the shapes.

4 triangles

2 triangles

4 triangles

8 triangles

Warm-Up 93

What's the Problem?

Work It Out

Evan drew a square with a perimeter of 4 centimeters.

1. **What is the perimeter of 2 connected squares?**

   _____

2. **What is the perimeter of 5 squares connected in a row?**

   _____

3. **Complete Evan's list by finding the perimeters.**

# of Squares	Perimeter
1	4 cm
2	
3	
4	
5	
6	
7	
8	

- -

Warm-Up 94

What's the Problem?

Work It Out

Evan drew a square with a perimeter of 12 centimeters.

1. **What is the perimeter of 2 connected squares?**

   _____

2. **What is the perimeter of 3 connected squares and 4 connected squares when connected in a row?**

   _____

   _____

Warm-Up
95

What's the Problem?

Work It Out

Michelle drew a series of geometric figures shown here. She wanted to identify the angles in each figure as acute angles (A), right angles (R), or obtuse angles (O).

Label the angles in each figure with A, R, or O.

1.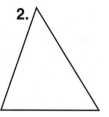

2.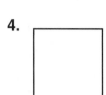

3.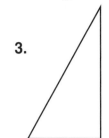

4.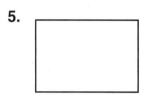

5.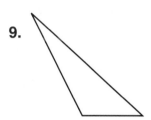

6.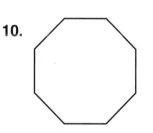

7.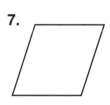

8.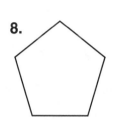

9.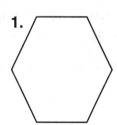

10.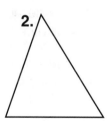

- -

Warm-Up
96

What's the Problem?

Work It Out

Michelle used a ruler to measure the sides of each figure she illustrated to the nearest half centimeter.

What is the perimeter of each figure? Write each answer inside the shape.

1.

2.

3.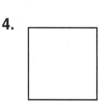

4.

5.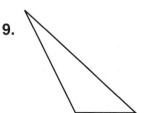

6.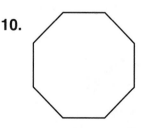

7.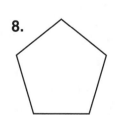

8.

9.

10.

Warm-Up 97

What's the Problem?   ## Work It Out

Patti drew as many diagonal lines from each vertex of a polygon to every other vertex of the polygon that she could.

Count the number of sides and vertices for each polygon.

How many diagonal lines can she draw in each of the polygons listed and illustrated in the chart?

Polygon	# of Sides	# of Vertices	# of Diagonal Lines
triangle			
square			
pentagon			
hexagon			
octagon			

- -

Warm-Up 98

What's the Problem?   ## Work It Out

Patti wondered what would be the number of sides, vertices, and diagonal lines for a decagon.

Find the correct number of sides, vertices, and diagonal lines.

_____

_____

_____

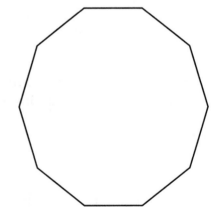

Warm-Up 99

What's the Problem?

Work It Out

Jordan drew a hexagon with a perimeter of 6 centimeters.

When connected in a row, what is the perimeter of 2, 3, 4, and 5 connected hexagons?

Complete the chart.

# of Hexagons	Perimeter
1	6 cm
2	
3	
4	
5	

- -

Warm-Up 100

What's the Problem?

Work It Out

1. **What is the pattern Jordan should find?**

   _____

2. **What would be the perimeter of 6 connected hexagons?**

   _____

3. **What would be the perimeter of 10 connected hexagons?**

   _____

What's the Problem?

Work It Out

Patrick knew that all triangles have a total of 180 degrees in their interior angles.

How many degrees do each of these equilateral triangles have in each angle?

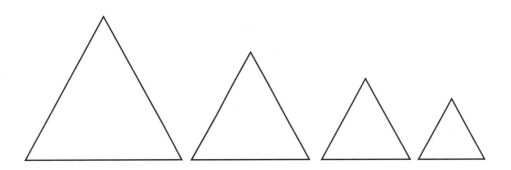

_____

What's the Problem?

Work It Out

Patrick knew that all isosceles right triangles have 1 right angle and 2 other equal sides and equal angles.

How many degrees are in each of the angles of these isosceles right triangles?

_____

Label the degrees on the triangles.

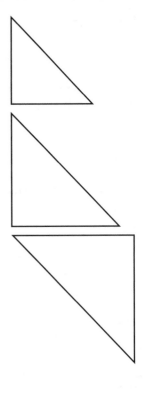

What's the Problem?

Work It Out

Joshua is building a doghouse for his new puppy. The floor is 6 feet long and 4 feet wide.

1. **What is the area of the floor in square feet?**

   _____

2. **How many wooden pieces 1 foot long and 1 foot wide would he need to cover the floor of the doghouse?**

   _____

· ·

What's the Problem?

Work It Out

Joshua is making each of the 2 sides of the doghouse 6 feet long and 3 feet high.

1. **What is the area of each side in square feet?**

   _____

2. **What is the area of the rear of the doghouse, which will be 4 feet long and 3 feet high?**

   _____

Warm-Up 105

What's the Problem?   **Work It Out**

Cory measured 1 square of a 64-square checkerboard.
It was 2 inches long and 2 inches wide. There were 8
squares in each row and column.

1. How long was the board?

_____

2. How wide was the board?

_____

3. What is the area of the board?

_____

4. What is the perimeter of the board?

_____

· ·

Warm-Up 106

What's the Problem?   **Work It Out**

Cory designed his own 64-square checkerboard
with squares 3 centimeters long and 3
centimeters wide. There were 8 squares in each
row and column.

1. What is the length of his board?

_____

2. What is the width of his board?

_____

3. What is the area of the board?

_____

4. What is the perimeter of the board?

_____

What's the Problem?   Work It Out

Catherine and Kevin got into an argument over who had the biggest, and therefore the best, bedroom. Their mother got tired of the arguing and told them to settle the argument by measuring each room and computing the area of each room.

1. **Kevin's room is 10 feet long and 8 feet wide. What is the area?**

   _____

2. **Catherine's room is 9 feet long and 9 feet wide. What is the area?**

   _____

3. **Which room is larger? What is the difference?**

   _____

• •

What's the Problem?   Work It Out

Catherine complained that she had less closet space than her brother, Kevin. She measured her closet, which is 8 feet long and 4 feet wide. Kevin measured his closet, which is 9 feet long and 3 feet wide.

1. **What is the area of each closet?**

   _____

   _____

2. **Who has the larger closet?**

   _____

Geometry: volume; multiplication; division

What's the Problem?   Work It Out

In August, Irene made a chocolate birthday cake with thick, white frosting for her little sister's birthday party. The cake was 3 inches high. It was 12 inches wide and 10 inches long.

1. **What was the volume of the cake in cubic inches?**

   _____

2. **Irene wanted to serve 6 cubic inches of cake to each of her little sister's friends. How many friends can she serve?**

   _____

- -

What's the Problem?   Work It Out

In September, Irene's mother and little sister made Irene's birthday cake. They made her chocolate cake with chocolate frosting. The whole cake was 4 inches high, 12 inches wide, and 12 inches long.

1. **What is the volume of her cake?**

   _____

2. **How many of Irene's friends can she serve 6 cubic inches of cake to?**

   _____

Geometry: volume; multiplication; division

What's the Problem?   Work It Out

Edwin was distracted during math class. He wondered how many cubic feet of air was available for breathing in his classroom, which was 32 feet long, 30 feet wide, and 12 feet high.

1. **What is the volume of air in the classroom in cubic feet (when the classroom is empty)?**

   _____

2. **There are 30 students in his classroom. How many cubic feet of air are available for each student?**

   _____

What's the Problem?   Work It Out

Edwin wondered if there was enough air in his school's multipurpose room, which was designed to hold 300 students. The multipurpose room is 100 feet long, 60 feet wide, and 30 feet high.

1. **What is the volume of the multipurpose room?**

   _____

2. **How many cubic feet of air does it hold (when the room is empty)?**

   _____

3. **How many cubic feet of air is available to each of the 300 students in the room when it is full?**

   _____

Warm-Up 113

What's the Problem?

Work It Out

Angela was studying the streets on her way to school. Elm Street and Maple Avenue crossed each other to make 4 equal corners.

1. Which quadrant is the school located in?

   _____

2. How many degrees is each angle (where the streets cross)?_____

3. Which 2 angles are adjacent to angle/ quadrant 2?

   _____

4. Which angle is opposite to angle/ quadrant 3?

   _____

5. What is the total number of degrees in the entire 4 angles?

   _____

```
                              |  • City Park
                              |
          Maple Ave.    2  |  1
          _____|_____
                          3  |  4
                              | Elm St.   • Sunnyvale
                              |              School
```

Warm-Up 114

What's the Problem?

Work It Out

Use the diagram to answer the questions.

1. Which quadrant is the park located in?

   _____

2. Name all angle pairs that together form a straight angle of 180 degrees.

   _____

   _____

3. Which angles are adjacent to angle/ quadrant 4?

   _____

4. Which angle is opposite to angle/ quadrant 4?

   _____

```
                              |  • City Park
                              |
          Maple Ave.    2  |  1
          _____|_____
                          3  |  4
                              | Elm St.   • Sunnyvale
                              |              School
```

Warm-Up 115

What's the Problem?

Work It Out

Paul was thinking about geometry as he walked to school. He knew that parallel lines remain the same distance apart and don't meet or get closer to each other. He knew that perpendicular lines intersect forming right angles. Skew lines don't intersect, but they are not parallel. Paul saw streets that were examples of each type of line.

1.

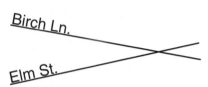

Grant Dr.

Label each of the street patterns below as perpendicular, parallel, skew, or intersecting but not perpendicular.

2.

Aspen St.

Walnut Ave.

3.

Birch Ln.

Elm St.

4.

River Dr.

Lake St.

• •

Warm-Up 116

What's the Problem?

Paul saw 2 straight streets that intersected but not at right angles. One angle is given.

What is the measure in degrees of angles A, B, and C?

_____

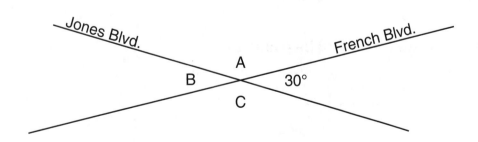

Jones Blvd.

French Blvd.

A

B

30°

C

Warm-Up 117

What's the Problem?   **Work It Out**

Anna planted and cared for a flower garden for her neighbor. The garden was shaped like a triangle. It was 5 feet on one side, 5 feet on a second side, and had a base of 8 feet.

1. **What was the perimeter of the garden?**

   _____

2. **What kind of triangle is created by the flower garden?**

   A. **scalene**

   B. **equilateral**

   C. **isosceles**

   D. **right**

• •

Warm-Up 118

What's the Problem?   **Work It Out**

In Anna's garden, the distance from the top of the triangle to the base was 4 feet.

1. **What was the area of the triangular flower garden in square feet?**

   _____

Anna's neighbor wanted the right half of the garden planted in daisies.

2. **How many square feet would be planted in daisies?**

   _____

What's the Problem?

Work It Out

Josiah's aunt paid him to help her fix her rectangular backyard, which was messy and full of weeds. She had him measure the length, which was 20 feet, and the width, which was 12 feet. She had him draw a line in the dirt from the top of the left side of the rectangle to the bottom of the right side.

1. **What is the exact name of the triangles formed by this line?**

   A. **equilateral**

   B. **isosceles**

   C. **right**

2. **Are the 2 triangles equal or unequal in area?**

   _____

What's the Problem?

Work It Out

Josiah's aunt agreed to pay him $3 a square foot for digging up the soil and planting one triangle with corn and peas.

1. **What is the area of the triangle in square feet?**

   _____

2. **How much will Josiah earn by planting that side of the garden?**

   _____

What's the Problem?   Work It Out

Melissa posed this riddle to her friends in the math club: "I am a quadrilateral, but I do not have any right angles. I have only 2 equal sides but I have 2 pairs of equal angles. What am I?"

What is the name of her geometric figure?
Draw diagrams to help you determine the figure.

_____

What's the Problem?   Work It Out

Jay posed this riddle to Melissa and his friends in the math club: "I am a quadrilateral and a parallelogram. I have 2 pairs of equal angles and 4 equal sides. I have no right angles. What am I?"

What is the name of his geometric figure?
Draw diagrams to help you determine the figure.

_____

What's the Problem?   **Work It Out**

The tetherball court assigned to Mildred's class is a circle with the pole in the middle. The chain holding the tetherball is 5 feet long. It is also the same length as the radius of that circle. Mildred wants to know how much space the court takes up.

What is the area of the circle?

_____

(formula for the area of a circle = πr²)

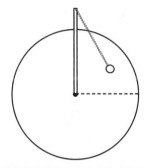

• •

Warm-Up
124

What's the Problem?   **Work It Out**

Mildred was curious about the distance around the tetherball court, the circumference of the circle.

What is the circumference of the tetherball court?

_____

(formula for the circumference of a circle = 2πr)

Warm-Up 125

What's the Problem?

Work It Out

Monique and Denise examined the section of their school that included the upper grades. They saw that it had a rectangular top, a rectangular bottom, and 4 rectangular sides. They wanted to know the name for that geometric figure.

1. **What is the name of the figure?**

   _____

2. **How many faces does the building have?**

   _____

3. **How many vertices (points) does the structure have?**

   _____

4. **How many edges (lines) does the figure have?**

   _____

Warm-Up 126

What's the Problem?

Work It Out

Monique and Denise used these plastic figures in science to show the 7 colors that make up white light.

1. **What is the name of this figure?**

   _____

2. **How many faces does the figure have?**

   _____

3. **How many vertices (points) does the prism have?**

   _____

4. **How many edges (lines) does the prism have?**

   _____

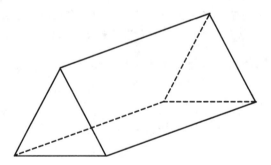

What's the Problem?

Work It Out

Alyssa loves the perfection of circles. She likes drawing them with a compass and working with them. She knows there are 360 degrees in a circle, which makes them easy to divide into equal parts.

1. How many degrees are in a half circle?

_____

2. How many degrees in a quarter circle?

_____

3. How many degrees in $\frac{1}{3}$ of a circle?

_____

4. How many degrees in $\frac{1}{6}$ of a circle?

_____

• •

What's the Problem?

Work It Out

Alyssa started a list of all the numbers that will divide evenly into 360 (the factors) and therefore can be used to create even segments of a circle.

1. Add every number pair you can to her list.

2. How many numbers will divide evenly into 360?

_____

(1, 360)

(2, 180)

Warm-Up 129

What's the Problem?

Work It Out

Juan Carlos drew this graph to illustrate the number of blocks he has been running and the number of minutes it takes.

1. **How many minutes did it take Juan Carlos to run 2 blocks?**

   _____

2. **How many minutes did it take him to run 6 blocks?**

   _____

3. **How many minutes would it likely take Juan Carlos to run 12 blocks?**

   _____

4. **What are the coordinates at point A?**

   _____

5. **What are the coordinates at point B?**

   _____

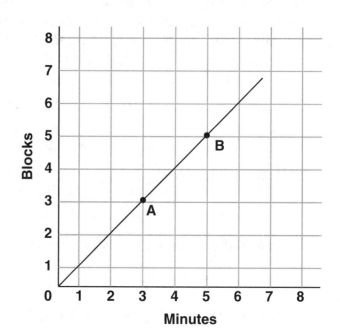

- -

Warm-Up 130

What's the Problem?

Work It Out

Juan Carlos made this graph to illustrate the location of places he liked.

1. **What are the coordinates of the ball field?**

   _____

2. **What are the coordinates of the park?**

   _____

3. **What are the coordinates of the school?**

   _____

4. **What are the coordinates of his home?**

   _____

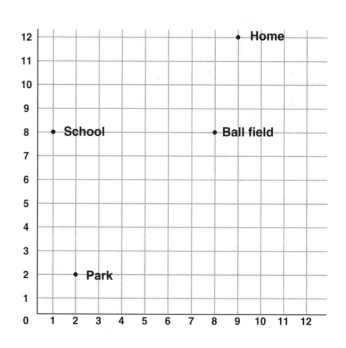

What's the Problem?   Work It Out

Julianna wanted to compare the width of a sheet of art paper in metric and U.S. units. She discovered that it was the length of 1 ruler, which is 1 foot, or 12 inches.

1. If 1 inch equeals about 2.5 centimeters, about how many centimeters equal the length of 1 foot?

_____

2. About how many centimeters equal the length of 1 yard?

_____

What's the Problem?   Work It Out

Julianna made a list of items that can be measured with inches or with centimeters.

Check whether the item is closer to an inch or a centimeter in length.

	Inch	Centimeter
small pencil eraser	_____	_____
eyelash	_____	_____
fingernail	_____	_____
width of little finger	_____	_____
quarter	_____	_____
thickness of a notebook	_____	_____
thickness of a math book	_____	_____
width of a pencil	_____	_____
width of an ear	_____	_____

What's the Problem?

Work It Out

Their teacher told Mary and Michael to measure the length and width of their classroom with a measuring tape. The length of the room is 30 feet and the width is 32 feet.

1. **What is the perimeter of their classroom?**

   _____

2. **What is the area of their classroom?**

   _____

• •

What's the Problem?

Work It Out

Mary and Michael asked the librarian if they could take measurements in the school library. They measured its width at 25 feet and its length at 36 feet.

1. **What is the perimeter of the library?**

   _____

2. **What is the area of the library?**

   _____

3. **Mary and Michael's classroom is 30 ft. by 32 ft. Is it bigger than the library?**

   _____

What's the Problem?   Work It Out

Sean and David designed and created their own
model rockets using vinegar and baking soda
for propellant, and a cork as the rocket fired
from a soda bottle. Sean measured the flight
of his rocket at 31 meters. David measured the
distance his rocket flew at 33 yards. They knew
that 1 meter equals about 39.37 inches.

1. Whose rocket had the longest flight?

_____

2. What was the difference in inches?

_____

• •

Warm-Up
136

What's the Problem?   Work It Out

Sean and David decided to try their experiment
again. They measured their ingredients carefully
and tried for longer distances. Sean measured
his flight at 32 meters this time. David's rocket
flew 34.5 yards.

1. Which rocket flew the farthest?

_____

**2. How many inches farther did the winning
      rocket fly?**

_____

Warm-Up 137

What's the Problem?   Work It Out

Joseph rode his bicycle 15 miles in 5 hours along a nice, level bike path in his community.

1. **How many miles did he travel in 1 hour?**

   _____

2. **At this rate, how many miles would he be able to travel in 4 hours?**

   _____

• •

Warm-Up 138

What's the Problem?   Work It Out

Joseph began preparing himself for a 20-mile bike-a-thon through the streets of his city. He hopes to finish in 5 hours or less.

How fast will he have to travel to ride the 20 miles in 5 hours?

_____

What's the Problem?

Work It Out

Jerry and his dad traveled 2,800 miles from San Francisco, California, to Washington, D.C., in 56 hours of driving time.

What was their average rate of speed in miles per hour?

_____

What's the Problem?

Work It Out

Jerry and his dad returned home from Washington, D.C., by airplane in 8 hours of flight time—a distance of 2,800 miles.

What was their average rate of speed in miles per hour?

_____

What's the Problem?

Work It Out

Brandon knew the distance from his school to his house was exactly 1 mile. He offered to save his mother time and the cost of gas by walking to and from school every day. In return, she offered to give him a dollar for every time he walked to or from school.

1. **How much money did Brandon get paid on his first 5-day school week?**

   _____

2. **In his first month of school, Brandon walked 18 days. How much did he get paid for 2 trips a day for 18 days?**

   _____

3. **If Brandon has perfect attendance for the 180 days of school, how much money could he earn in a school year?**

   _____

What's the Problem?

Work It Out

Brandon knew there are 5,280 feet in 1 mile, which equals 1,760 yards.

1. **How many feet did he walk to and from school the first 5 days?**

   _____

2. **How many yards did he walk to and from school that week?**

   _____

3. **Brandon counted 2,500 footsteps on his the way to school. How many footsteps would that be in 5 complete trips to and from school?**

   _____

Warm-Up 143

What's the Problem?   Work It Out

Charlie wants to be like his older brother and join the track team when he gets to high school. He keeps in shape by running everywhere he can. He ran to the library, which is 2 miles from his home, and then he ran back home with the books.

1. **How many feet did Charlie run to and from the library?**

   _____

2. **How many yards did he run to and from the library?**

   _____

Warm-Up 144

What's the Problem?   Work It Out

It took Charlie 23 minutes to run to the library and 29 minutes to run back from the library.

What was Charlie's average number of minutes per mile?

_____

What's the Problem?

Work It Out

On the first day of school, September 4th, Bryan was already thinking of his winter vacation. He is going to go skiing with his uncle in Canada. His vacation starts on December 19, and he is very excited.

1. Not counting the first day of school, how many more days is it until Bryan's winter vacation starts?

_____

2. How many weeks do those days equal?

_____

- -

What's the Problem?

Work It Out

Bryan needed to make a calendar of the year to see how many days there are from September 4 (the first day of school) until summer vacation began on June 21.

1. Complete his yearly calendar of days. (Hint: this is not a leap year.)

2. Total days for the year = _____

3. Total days until summer vacation = _____

September	=	30 days
October	=	31 days
November	=	
December	=	
January	=	
February	=	
March	=	
April	=	
May	=	
June	=	

Warm-Up
147

What's the Problem?

Work It Out

Alan wanted to hang around with his older sister, Arlene, and her high school friends. Arlene didn't want Alan there so she thought of a way to keep him out of their way for a while. She offered to pay him 1 penny for every number he counted—if he counted to 10,000. He had to write each number in a list as proof of counting. He couldn't talk to his sister until he had finished and had the proof.

She didn't have 10,000 pennies, but she was sure Alan would quit and leave them alone for a while. Alan knew she didn't have the money, but he wanted to see what she would do when he actually did the counting.

If he counted 1 number each second, how many hours, minutes, and seconds did it take Alan to count to 10,000?

_____

Warm-Up
148

What's the Problem?

Work It Out

When Alan finished counting to 10,000, he took the list to Arlene and demanded his money. She got angry because she didn't believe he would actually finish and she didn't have the pennies. Alan took the papers to his mom and explained the deal. She called in Arlene who admitted she had no money. Alan's mom paid him in cash, not pennies, and told Arlene she would have to pay her back with chores paid at $2 an hour.

1. **How much money, in dollars, did Alan collect?**

   _____

2. **How many hours of chores did Arlene owe her mom?**

   _____

What's the Problem?   Work It Out

Rhonda was doing a simple science experiment. She carefully placed 1 drop of red food coloring into 1 cup of water. She dropped another drop into a quart of water. She dropped a third drop into a gallon of water. She observed the results.

1. How many ounces of water are in 1 cup?

_____

2. How many ounces of water are in 1 quart?

_____

3. How many ounces of water are in 1 gallon?

_____

What's the Problem?   Work It Out

Rhonda wanted to know which container held more—a quart or a liter. She carefully poured exactly four 8-ounce cups of water into the quart bottle. She then carefully poured the same amount of water into the liter bottle. She found that the liter bottle had room to hold about 2 more ounces of water.

1. How many ounces of water went into the quart bottle?

_____

2. How many ounces of water could the liter bottle have held?

_____

3. What percentage of water is in the liter bottle?

_____

What's the Problem?   **Work It Out**

Christopher drew a perfect square exactly 1 foot long
on each side. His ruler was exactly one inch wide and
he drew lines 1 inch apart down the length of his square
dividing it into 12 equal spaces. He then turned the paper
and drew lines one inch apart going the opposite way.

1. **How many 1-inch squares did he make in his
   large square?**

   _____

2. **How many 1-inch squares are in $\frac{1}{4}$ of a square foot?**

   _____

3. **How many 1-inch squares are in $\frac{1}{2}$ of a square foot?**

   _____

4. **How many 1-inch squares are in $\frac{1}{12}$ of a square foot?**

   _____

What's the Problem?   **Work It Out**

Christopher took a large piece of paper and drew
a square exactly 1 yard long and 1 yard wide.
He drew straight lines down the large square at
the 1-foot point and 2-foot point. He then did the
same going across.

1. **How many squares 1 foot long and 1 foot
   wide are there in 1 square yard?**

   _____

2. **How many 1-inch squares could be
   drawn in 1 square yard?**

   _____

Warm-Up 153

What's the Problem?

Samantha made a list of some common measurements for length, weight, and volume, and another list of things to help her visualize those measurements when she hears them.

Help Samantha match the mathematical unit of measurement with the item that best represents the measurement.

Work It Out

Unit of Measurement	Reminder
1 centimeter	distance a car travels in 5 minutes
1 inch	length of a small paper clip
1 foot	width of your little finger
1 yard	a medium-sized drink
1 meter	weight of a slice of bread
1 mile	a small container of milk
1 gram	weight of a large potato
1 ounce	a large container of gasoline
1 pound	width of a front door
1 pint	height of a kindergartener
1 quart	a bit longer than a sheet of paper
1 gallon	weight of a penny

Warm-Up 154

What's the Problem?

Samantha's classmate Sara is having difficulty making up a list of her own measurement reminders.

Help Sara make up some reminders for the given measurements.

Work It Out

1 centimeter = _____

1 inch = _____

1 foot = _____

1 yard = _____

1 mile = _____

1 pound = _____

1 pint = _____

1 quart = _____

1 gallon = _____

What's the Problem?

Work It Out

Joanne had 8 bottles of water to use in a science project. Each bottle held 250 milliliters of water. She also had an eyedropper that can hold about 1 milliliter of liquid.

1. **How many milliliters of water did she have altogether?**

   _____

2. **How many eyedroppers could she fill with water?**

   _____

3. **How many liters of water did Joanne have?**

   _____

· ·

What's the Problem?

Work It Out

Joanne did an evaporation science project where she mixed 10 milliliters of food coloring, 50 milliliters of cooking oil, 300 milliliters of vinegar, and 500 milliliters of water and set them outside.

1. **How many more milliliters of liquid would Joanne need to make 1 liter?**

   _____

When she collected the remaining mixture at the end of a hot day, Joanne had 0.5 liters of liquid.

2. **How many milliliters are in 0.5 liters?**

   _____

3. **How many milliliters had evaporated?**

   _____

What's the Problem?

Work It Out

Jeffrey rode his bicycle from his home to his grandmother's farm, which was a distance of 8 miles. He took 2 hours to make the ride. On the way home, Jeffrey took a detour that made his return trip 10 miles long. It took him $2\frac{1}{2}$ hours to get home.

1. **What was his rate of speed to the farm in miles per hour?**

   _____

2. **What was his rate of speed to get back home in miles per hour?**

   _____

What's the Problem?

Work It Out

Jeffrey's dad drove from Los Angeles to San Francisco—a distance of 400 miles—in 8 hours. His dad made the return trip in only 6 hours.

1. **What was his rate of speed to San Francisco in miles per hour?**

   _____

2. **What was his rate of speed to Los Angeles in miles per hour?**

   _____

What's the Problem?   Work It Out

Jeremiah rode his skateboard to his friend's house in another part of the neighborhood almost a mile away. It was 5,000 feet from Jeremiah's home, and he traveled the distance in 10 minutes.

What was Jeremiah's skateboarding speed in feet per minute?

_____

What's the Problem?   Work It Out

Jeremiah rode in a bicycle race to raise funds for victims of an earthquake. He rode 20 miles in 5 hours.

What was his rate of speed in miles per hour?

_____

What's the Problem?

Work It Out

Colleen was learning about angles in her math class. She looked around the room to see what things formed angles. She noticed that the opened doors, books on the shelf, her arms, folded papers, body postures, and crayons coloring all formed angles. Colleen tried to copy some of the angles by drawing them to the right.

Since Colleen lost her protractor, measure each angle for her and label its type.

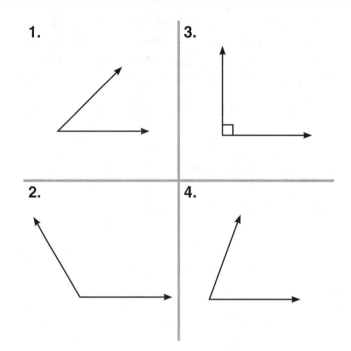

1.

2.

3.

4.

- -

What's the Problem?

Work It Out

On Thursday, Colleen's homework was to draw 1 right angle, 2 acute angles, and 2 obtuse angles.

Draw these angles for Colleen to use as examples.

What's the Problem?

Work It Out

Hannah noticed that the hands on a clock form different angles at different times. She wondered what angles were formed at the different meal times throughout the day. Hannah eats breakfast at 8:00 A.M., lunch at 1:00 P.M., after-school snack at 3:00 P.M., and dinner at 6:30 P.M.

What angles are formed at Hannah's meal times?

_____

_____

_____

_____

What's the Problem?

Work It Out

Hannah decided to use her knowledge of angles and time to try to trick her brother. One Saturday when he asked what they were doing that day, she said, "We are going to the movies at 135° then having lunch at 60°. Later we are going to Grandma's at 30° for an early dinner. We'll be home by 90° for bed."

If the minute hand is always on either "12" or "6," at what times are Hannah and her brother doing each of these things?

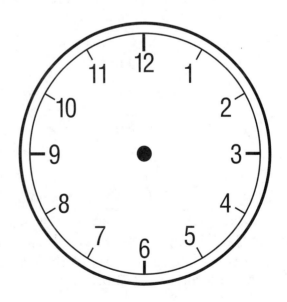

_____

_____

_____

_____

What's the Problem?

Work It Out

Ethan opened a small bag of color-coated candies. There were 30 candies in the bag. There were 6 blue-coated candies, 9 red candies, 12 brown candies, 2 orange candies, and 1 green candy. He made this chart to compare the blue candies to the total candies.

6 to 30 or 1 to 5	use "to"
6 : 30 or 1 : 5	use a colon
6/30 or 1/5	use a fraction
0.2	use a decimal
20%	use percent

Use Ethan's different ways of comparing to compare the red candies to the total and the brown candies to the total.

- -

What's the Problem?

Work It Out

Ethan made the list below to compare the blue candies to the red using ratios.

6 to 9 or 2 to 3
6 : 9 or 2 : 3
6/9 or 2/3
0.67
67%

Make a list to compare the blue candies to the brown and the orange to the brown candies using the different ways Ethan did.

Warm-Up 167

What's the Problem?   ## Work It Out

Irene computed the ratio of girls to students in her classroom. There were 16 girls and 28 total students in her class. She used the most common forms of expressing ratios.

1. **Compute the ratio of boys to the class using the colon and the fraction form of ratio.**

   _____

   _____

2. **Compute the ratio of boys to girls in the class using the colon and the fraction form of ratio.**

   _____

   _____

Girls to Entire Class

16 : 28 or 4 : 7

16/28 or 4/7

Warm-Up 168

What's the Problem?   ## Work It Out

Irene wanted to know the ratio of girls in her elementary school to the entire school population. There were 260 girls in a population of 510 students.

1. **What is the ratio of girls to the entire population?**

   _____

2. **What is the ratio of girls to boys?**

   _____

What's the Problem?   **Work It Out**

Angela ran 9 laps in 30 minutes during the Middlebrook Elementary School jogathon. Ellen jogged 10 laps. Ricardo jogged 14 laps and Tommy ran 11 laps. Linda ran the farthest, finishing 15 laps. Each lap was 250 feet long.

1. How many feet did each child run?

_____

_____

_____

_____

_____

2. What was the total number of feet run by all 5 children?

_____

What's the Problem?   **Work It Out**

Middlebrook Elementary School's jogathon had 563 participants who ran 4,954 laps altogether. Each lap was 250 feet long.

1. How many feet did the participants run altogether?

_____

2. How many miles of running did that equal? (Reminder: 1 mile = 5,280 feet)

_____

3. What was the average number of laps run during the jogathon?

_____

Warm-Up 171

What's the Problem?

Work It Out

Kenneth was looking to see which colleges would have money to loan or give to students to attend their college. The bar graph shows the endowment money available at 7 universities in billions of dollars.

1. **Which college has the most money to offer? How much money do they have?** _____

2. **Which college has about 5 times as much available money as College F?**

   _____

3. **Which college has the second most money to loan?** _____

4. **Which college has about half as much money as College A?** _____

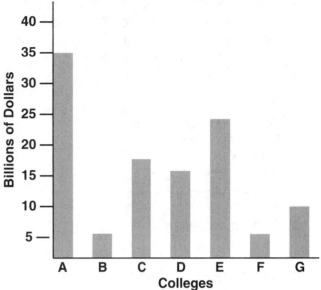

- -

Warm-Up 172

What's the Problem?

Work It Out

Kenneth found that tuition costs in college were about $14,000 a year for a four-year college and living expenses for food and the dormitory were about $8,000 a year. Expenses for tuition were rising at about $1,000 a year and about $500 a year for room and board.

Create a double bar graph to show the rise of tuition and the rise of room and board expenses over a 5-year period.

Use one color for tuition (T) and another color for room and board (R).

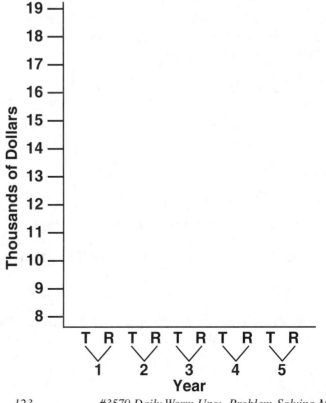

Warm-Up 173

What's the Problem?

Work It Out

Dana was interested in the maximum life spans of different creatures. She made this bar graph to represent the longest time that an individual could or did live. Dana is looking for the creature with the longest possible lifespan.

1. **Which listed creature lives the longest?** _____

2. **Which creature has the shortest lifespan?** _____

3. **Which creature lives to about 45 years?** _____

4. **Which creature lives 50 years or slightly more?** _____

5. **About how old can a condor live to be?** _____

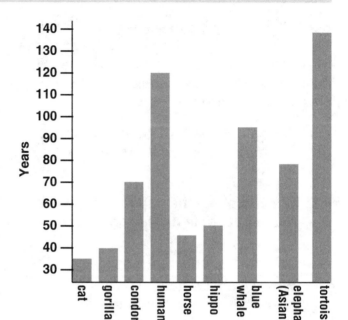

- -

Warm-Up 174

What's the Problem?

Work It Out

After a school trip to the zoo, Dana kept a tally showing the number of animals she counted in the first 5 areas she visited.

Monkeys	ЖHT ЖHT II
Elephants	ЖHT II
Lions	ЖHT I
Zebras	ЖHT ЖHT I
Gorillas	ЖHT IIII

1. **Record this information on a bar graph.**

2. **Which animal did she count half a dozen of?**

   _____

3. **What is the average number of animals she counted in each area?**

   _____

Warm-Up 175

What's the Problem?

Rita read the following table of bones in the human body. She wanted to know about how many bones were located in the different parts of the body.

1. About how many bones are located in the head?

   _____

2. About how many bones are located between the neck and waist?

   _____

3. About how many bones are located in the waist or below?

   _____

4. What is the total number of bones in the human body?

   _____

Work It Out

Bone Location	Number
Skull	22
Ears	6
Thorax	25
Vertebral column	24
Throat	1
Shoulder girdle	4
Arms + Hands	60
Pelvis	4
Legs + Feet	60

Warm-Up 176

What's the Problem?

Rita wanted to know what exercise was best for burning calories. In her research, she found this graph.

1. Which exercise was best for burning calories? How many did it burn?

   _____

2. How many calories were burned by 1 hour of walking? _____

3. How many calories were burned by 1 hour of playing tennis? _____

4. How many calories could Rita burn by bicycling for 3 hours? _____

5. How many calories could be burned by playing handball for 2 hours? _____

Work It Out

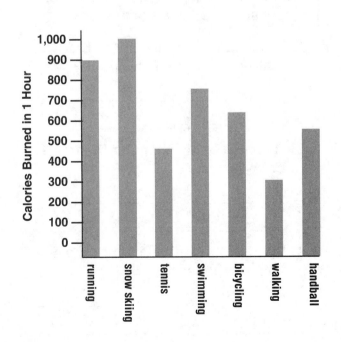

Warm-Up
177

What's the Problem?

Work It Out

Linda made a graph to illustrate her scores for the first 10 spelling tests of the year.

1. **For which test did Linda probably not study enough?**

   _____

2. **How many of her tests were either 90% or 100%?**

   _____

3. **What was her average grade over 10 weeks?**

   _____

4. **What can you learn about Linda's spelling grades from the graph?**

   _____

   _____

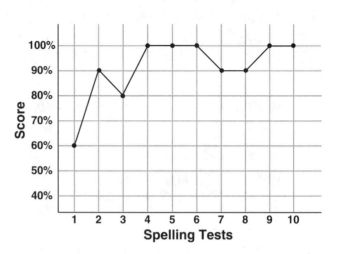

- -

Warm-Up
178

What's the Problem?

Work It Out

Linda made a graph to illustrate her scores for the first 10 math tests of the year.

1. **What can you know about Linda's math grades from the graph?**

   _____

   _____

2. **What probably changed the trend of her graph?**

   _____

   _____

3. **What probably happened on the 10th math test?**

   _____

   _____

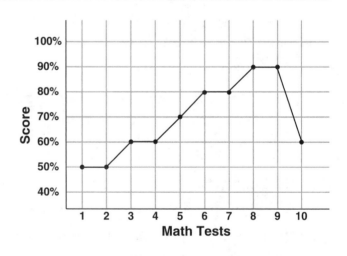

Warm-Up 179

What's the Problem?

Work It Out

Walter plotted these points on the grid. He wanted to use the grid as a board game to play with his math buddies. He told each player to label the ships at the proper coordinates.

The gunship is at (1, 7).

The destroyer is at (9, 6).

The submarine is at (6, 4).

The aircraft carrier is at (7, 9).

The battleship is at (7, 1).

You are Player 1. Label each ship at its proper coordinate.

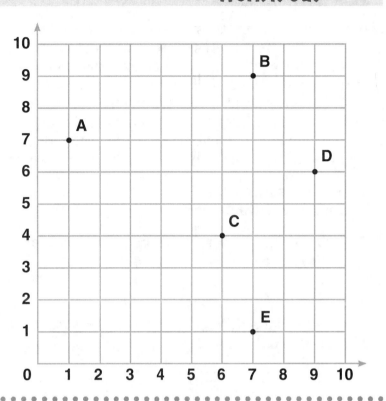

• •

Warm-Up 180

What's the Problem?

Work It Out

Walter rearranged the ships in his game so that all of them moved 3 spaces to the right and 1 space down.

Give the new coordinates for each ship.

	Old	New
Gunship	(1, 7)	
Destroyer	(5, 6)	
Submarine	(6, 4)	
Aircraft carrier	(7, 9)	
Battleship	(7, 1)	

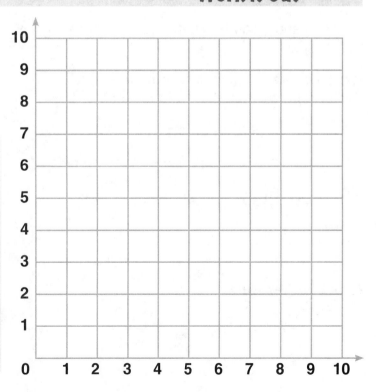

Warm-Up
181

What's the Problem?

Work It Out

Madison and Heather did an evaporation project for the school science fair. They mixed 1 gallon of water, 6 ounces of food coloring, and 8 ounces of salt in a flat pan 30 millimeters deep and placed it outside in the open where the hot sun would speed up evaporation. Heather and Madison checked the height daily and recorded the number of millimeters of the water level. They made a line graph to record the change over time.

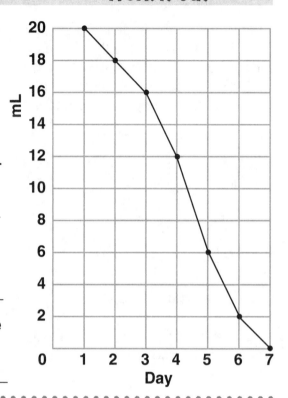

1. What was the general
   trend of the water level? _____

2. Why did the water level probably drop so far
   on the 5th day?

   _____

3. What was the difference in water level from the
   first day to the fifth day?

   _____

Warm-Up
182

What's the Problem?

Work It Out

Madison and Heather recorded this data on a graph from a science experiment.

Which of the following information is most likely to be recorded on this graph?

   A. the weights of different animals

   B. changes in temperature over 1 week

   C. a pattern of hair growth

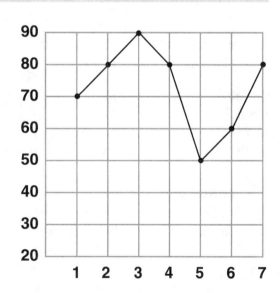

Give your reasons.

_____

_____

Warm-Up
183

What's the Problem?   ## Work It Out

Frances and Audrey took a survey about television-watching habits. They recorded the number of hours watched by fifth graders during the course of a week and recorded the information on the line plot below.

1. How many students did Frances and Audrey survey? _____

2. How many students watched 35 or more hours of TV? _____

3. How many students didn't watch any TV? _____

4. How many students watched TV 10 hours or less? _____

5. How many students watched between 15 and 20 hours of TV? _____

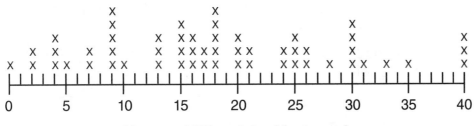

Hours of TV watched in 1 week

Warm-Up
184

What's the Problem?   ## Work It Out

Frances and Audrey were in charge of keeping track of how many laps the students ran during the fitness test. They made the list below.

# of Students	Laps Ran
5	10
1	15
3	12
4	13
5	8
2	6

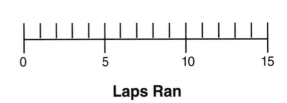

Laps Ran

1. Record the information on the line plot.

2. How many students participated in the fitness test? _____

3. How many students ran less than 10 laps? _____

4. How many total laps were run? _____

Warm-Up
185

What's the Problem?

Work It Out

Harvey and Jonathan took a survey of television preferences from all fifth graders in their school. They recorded their findings on the pictograph. Each student named his or her 2 favorite types of television programs.

1. **Which programming was the most favored by students? How many votes did it get?**

   _____

2. **How many votes did old movies receive?** _____

3. **Which 2 types of programs tied? How many votes did each receive?**

   _____

4. **What can you tell about fifth graders' program preferences from this pictograph?** _____

Favorite Television Programs

News ▪

Reality Shows ▫ ▫ ▫

Music Videos ▫ ▫ ▫ ▫ ▫ ▫ ▫

Comedy Shows ▫

Serious Drama ▪

Old Movies ▫ ▫

Talent Shows ▫ ▫ ▫ ▫

Key: Each full ▫ represents 8 votes.

• •

Warm-Up
186

What's the Problem?

Work It Out

1. **Conduct a class survey about favorite TV programs and record the results on the tally chart. Then create a pictograph using the data. Use a symbol to represent a number of votes.**

TV Programs	Student Votes
News	
Reality Shows	
Music Videos	
Comedy Shows	
Serious Drama	
Old Movies	
Talent Shows	

2. **How many votes did talent shows receive?** _____

3. **Which program type did the students like best?** _____

Key: Each _____ represents _____ votes

Warm-Up 187

What's the Problem?

Work It Out

Priscilla and Pamela interviewed the first 100 students they met on the playground and asked them to name their favorite fast food dinner. They recorded the collected information on the circle graph.

1. **Which food was preferred by most students?**

   _____

2. **Which 2 foods were not preferred by many students?**

   _____

3. **Which 2 foods together were preferred by over $\frac{2}{3}$ of the students interviewed?**

   _____

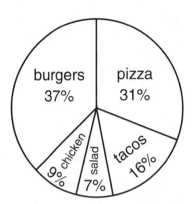

- -

Warm-Up 188

What's the Problem?

Work It Out

Pamela's sister, Patty, decided to survey her classmates to see what their favorite foods are out of 5 food choices. She listed her results in the chart to the right.

1. **Create a circle graph to represent the information in the chart.**

2. **How many students did Patty survey?**

   _____

3. **What is the favorite food of 50% of the class?**

   _____

4. **What is the favorite food of 25% of the class?**

   _____

Students	Favorite Foods
16	tacos
2	hamburgers
4	pizza
8	macaroni & cheese
2	chicken nuggets

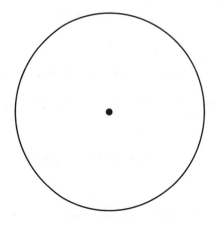

Warm-Up
189

What's the Problem?

Work It Out

Raphael adopted a puppy from a shelter. He cared for it and fed it very well. Raphael kept a record of its weight each week to the nearest pound. He kept a graph showing its weight for a 10-week period.

1. **What is the general trend of the puppy's growth?**

   _____

   _____

2. **How many pounds did the puppy grow over the 9 weeks following Week 1?**

   _____

3. **Between which weeks did the puppy's weight remain the same the longest?**

   _____

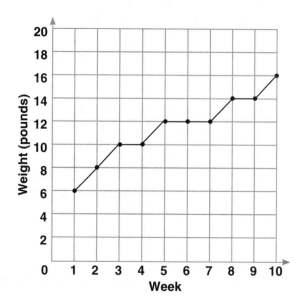

Warm-Up
190

What's the Problem?

Work It Out

Raphael planted some sunflower seeds and waited for them to sprout out of the soil. He kept a list of the tallest sunflowers' height over a period of 10 weeks.

Week	Height (in.)	Week	Height (in.)
1	5	6	65
2	15	7	80
3	25	8	90
4	40	9	95
5	50	10	100

1. **Record this information in a line graph.**

2. **What is the average growth rate per week?**

   _____

3. **At which week was it 7.5 feet tall?**

   _____

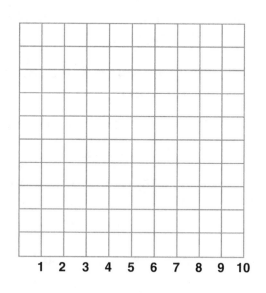

Warm-Up 191

What's the Problem?

Work It Out

Adriana and Brittany were playing a game using a spinner with 4 equal spaces. If a player spun a 3, the player got to double her score and then spin again.

1. **What is the probability of a player spinning a 3?**

   _____

2. **What is the probability of not spinning a 3?**

   _____

3. **What is the probability of spinning a 1?**

   _____

4. **What is the probability of spinning a 2, 3, or 4?**

   _____

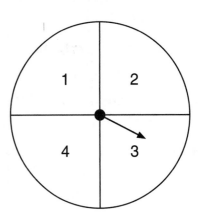

. . . .

Warm-Up 192

What's the Problem?

Work It Out

Adriana and Brittany used a spinner while playing a game. The spinner had 8 equal spaces. If a player spun an 8, she got to double her points and spin again. If she spun a 4, she lost one turn. If she spun a 5, she got an extra 50 points. If she spun a 7 or a 2, she had to lose all of her points and start again.

1. **What is the probability of spinning an 8?**

   _____

2. **What is the probability of not spinning either a 7 or a 2?**_____

3. **What is the probability of not spinning an 8?**

   _____

4. **Do you have a better chance of spinning a 5 or an 8?** _____

5. **What is the probability of spinning a 4, 2, or 7?** _____

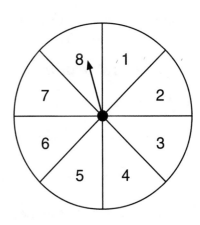

Warm-Up 193

What's the Problem?

Work It Out

Frances has her name in a classroom raffle for a large poster of her favorite entertainer. There were 9 other names in the drawing.

1. **What is the probability that her name will be drawn?** _____

2. **What is the probability that her name will not be drawn?** _____

Frances' name was not drawn. By the time the second drawing came around, Frances had her name in the drawing twice, along with 14 other names.

3. **What is the probability that Frances' name will be drawn this time?**_____

4. **What is the probability that her name will not be drawn?** _____

Warm-Up 194

What's the Problem?

Work It Out

The classroom raffle was expanded to include 3 identical posters for prizes. There were 40 tickets in the basket. Frances had her name on 4 tickets. Her best friend, Erica, has 2 tickets in the raffle.

For the first raffle prize, what is the probability that . . .

1. **Frances will have her name drawn?** _____

2. **Erica will have her name drawn?**_____

3. **Frances will not have her name drawn?** _____

4. **Erica will not have her name drawn?** _____

5. **either Erica or Frances will have her name drawn?** _____

6. **neither Frances nor Erica will have her name drawn?** _____

What's the Problem?   ## Work It Out

Javier flipped a dime 50 times. He recorded heads or tails after each flip.

1. **Most likely, how many times would the dime land on heads?**

   _____

2. **Most likely, how many times would the dime land on tails?**

   _____

3. **What is the probability of a dime landing on either heads or tails?**

   _____

4. **What is the probability of a dime landing on neither heads nor tails?**

   _____

· ·

Warm-Up 196

What's the Problem?   ## Work It Out

Number the back of your paper from 1 to 40. Flip a coin 40 times and record your results. Experimental probability often does not exactly track with theoretical probability.

1. **Most likely, how many times would the coin land on heads?** _____

2. **How many times did your coin land on heads?** _____

3. **Were you above or below the likely number of times? Were you close?**

   _____

Flip the coin another 40 times. Record your results.

4. **Did your total heads and total tails get closer to 1 in 2 (50%) or did they get further away?**

   _____

What's the Problem?

Work It Out

Stephanie conducted a class survey of preferences. She discovered that 30% of the students she questioned preferred chocolate sundaes for dessert and 60% preferred playing basketball at recess.

1. **What is the probability that a student preferred both chocolate sundaes for dessert and playing basketball at recess?**

   _____

2. **What is the probability that a student preferred neither chocolate sundaes for dessert nor playing basketball at recess?**

   _____

What's the Problem?

Work It Out

The results of Stephanie's survey showed that 20% of the students she questioned preferred cherry pie for dessert and 15% preferred playing handball at recess.

1. **What is the probability that a student preferred both cherry pie for dessert and playing handball at recess?**

   _____

2. **What is the probability that a student preferred neither cherry pie for dessert nor playing handball at recess?**

   _____

What's the Problem?

Work It Out

Sara and Valerie are twins. They have their names in a drawing with 8 other students for "Students of the Week" in the upper grades at their school. Two names are always drawn. They didn't care whose name was drawn first, but they both wanted their names drawn.

1. **What is the probability that one of the 2 twins' names will be drawn first?**

   _____

2. **If one twin's name is drawn first, what is the probability that the other twin's name will be drawn second?**

   _____

3. **What is the probability that both names will be drawn first and second?**

   _____

- -

What's the Problem?

Work It Out

Sarah and Valerie have their names in a drawing with a total of 20 names. Two names will be chosen. The winners get to go out to lunch with the teacher.

1. **What is the probability that one of the 2 girls' names will be drawn first?**

   _____

2. **If one girl's name is drawn first, what is the probability that the other girl's name will be drawn second?**

   _____

3. **What is the probability that both names will be drawn first and second?**

   _____

What's the Problem?   **Work It Out**

Dana and Sergio were playing a game with a 6-sided die. A roll of 5 entitled the player to roll again. Rolling a 3 meant the player lost a turn.

1. **What is the probability of a player getting to roll again?**

   _____

2. **What is the probability of a player having to lose a turn?**

   _____

3. **What is the probability of not rolling a 5?**

   _____

• •

What's the Problem?   **Work It Out**

In a dice game with a 6-sided die, Dana and Sergio could earn 20 points if they rolled a 1 or a 6. They lost 10 points if they rolled a 2, 3, or 5. They rolled again if they rolled a 4.

1. **What is the probability of a player earning 20 points in one roll?**

   _____

2. **What is the probability of a player losing 10 points in one roll?**

   _____

3. **What is the probability of not rolling a 2, 3, or 5 in one roll?**

   _____

4. **What is the probability of a player getting to roll again in one roll?**

   _____

Warm-Up 203

What's the Problem?

Work It Out

Troy and Tracy are rolling 2 regular dice in a board game. They want to know what total is most likely to come up on a roll. They have started a list of possible outcomes.

1. **Complete the list of possible outcomes.**

2. **What is the total number of possible outcomes (rolls of the dice)?**

   _____

Total	Numbers
2	1 + 1
3	1 + 2
4	2 + 2, 3 + 1
5	4 + 1,
6	
7	
8	
9	
10	
11	
12	

• •

Warm-Up 204

What's the Problem?

Work It Out

Use Troy and Tracy's list above to answer the following questions.

1. **What is the probability of either Troy or Tracy rolling a total of 2?**

   _____

2. **What is the probability of rolling a total of 4?**

   _____

3. **What is the probability of rolling a total of 7?**

   _____

4. **What is the probability of rolling a total of 1?**

   _____

5. **Which totals have the highest probability of being rolled?** _____

6. **Which 4 totals have the lowest probability of being rolled?** _____

7. **What is the combined probability of rolling either a total of 6 or 7?** _____

Warm-Up
205

What's the Problem?

Work It Out

David, Bryan, Annette, and Angela are playing a simple card game with a full deck of 52 cards. Every deck of cards has 4 suits, or symbols: diamonds, hearts, clubs, and spades. For each symbol, there are cards with numbers 2 through 10, a jack, a queen, a king, and an ace. The 4 friends are taking turns picking a card to see who gets the highest value.

1. **What is the probability of a player picking a king?**

   _____

2. **What is the probability of a player picking a diamond?**

   _____

3. **What is the probability of a player picking a 2 of hearts?**

   _____

Warm-Up
206

What's the Problem?

Work It Out

David and Bryan are using one complete deck of cards to play a game in which 21 is the winning score. Picture cards are worth 10 points. Aces are worth 11 points. Number cards are worth face value. David has a 10 and a queen. Bryan has a jack. He needs an ace to win.

1. **What is the probability of Bryan drawing an ace from the remaining cards in the deck?**

   _____

2. **What is the probability that Bryan will draw a card worth 10 points from the remaining cards to tie David?**

   _____

What's the Problem?

Work It Out

Adreena and Arlene measured the height of 6 girls in their class. They recorded the information on the graph.

1. **Which student is 4 feet tall?**

   _____

2. **Which students are the closest in height? How close are they?**

   _____

   _____

3. **What is the average height in inches of all the girls?**

   _____

4. **What is the range between the tallest and the shortest girl?**

   _____

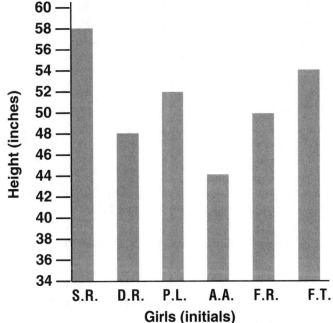

- -

What's the Problem?

Work It Out

Measure the height of 5 classmates of the same gender. Record the information on a bar graph and answer the questions below.

1. **Which students are the closest in height? How close are they?**

   _____

   _____

2. **What is the average height in inches of all the students?**

   _____

3. **What is the range between the tallest and the shortest student?**

   _____

Warm-Up 209

What's the Problem?

Yvonne and Briana used a yardstick to measure the snowfall during a blizzard that lasted for several hours. They took measurements every 1 to 2 hours from morning until it stopped.

1. **How many inches of snow did they measure at hours 3 and 4?**

   _____

2. **How many inches did they measure at their final measurement?** _____

3. **When did the snow stop falling?**

   _____

4. **Between which hours did the snow fall the fastest?**

   _____

Work It Out

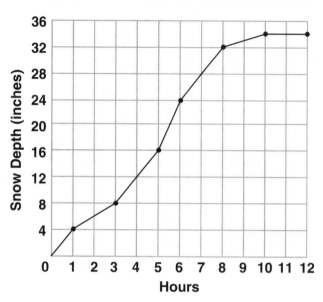

- -

Warm-Up 210

What's the Problem?

Yvonne and Briana measured the amount of snow remaining on the ground after a blizzard. The graph illustrates the amount of snow that melted every day for 5 days afterwards.

1. **How many inches of snow melted the first day?**

   _____

2. **Between which days did the most snow melt?**

   _____

3. **By day 5, how many total inches had melted?**

   _____

4. **How many more inches of snow still need to melt for it to be all gone?**

   _____

Work It Out

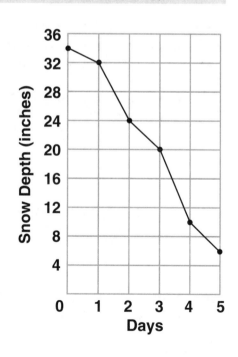

Warm-Up 211

What's the Problem?

Work It Out

Saul has been saving money to buy a skateboard. He needs $53 to buy the board he wants. He has saved $17. If he saves his money to buy a fancier, faster board, the cost would be $84.

1. **Solve this equation to find how much more money Saul needs for the cheaper board.**

   n + $17 = $53

   _____

2. **Solve this equation to find how much more money Saul needs to buy the faster board.**

   n + $17 = $84

   _____

• •

Warm-Up 212

What's the Problem?

Work It Out

If Saul used the money to buy a 10-speed bike, he would need $196 total. If he used the money to buy a used skateboard, he would need $13 more.

1. **Write an equation and solve it to determine how much more money he needs to buy a 10-speed bike.**

   _____

2. **Write an equation and solve it to determine how much the used skateboard would cost.**

   _____

Warm-Up 213

What's the Problem?

Work It Out

Paul collects comic books with his favorite stories. He also trades and sells some comics. On Monday, he had 44 comics. He traded away 4 comics and received 6 in return. On Tuesday, he bought 6 new comics and sold 4 comics. His dad gave him 11 comics on Wednesday.

1. **Solve the equation to determine how many comics he now has.**

   $$44 - 4 + 6 + 6 - 4 + 11 = n$$

   _____

2. **How many comics did Paul have after he added 13 comics to his collection and sold 6 comics? Write an equation to illustrate the problem and then solve it.**

   _____

Warm-Up 214

What's the Problem?

Work It Out

Paul had 100 comics on the Monday before school began. During the week, he bought 16 comics, sold 11 comics, and was given 22 comics.

1. **Write an equation to illustrate his gains and losses. Solve the equation.**

   _____

2. **Write an equation to illustrate only his buying and selling of comics. Solve the equation.**

   _____

Warm-Up 215

What's the Problem?

Work It Out

Alex bought 4 music CDs by his favorite artist and 3 DVDs starring his favorite actor. Each CD cost $20 and each DVD cost $15. He wrote an equation to illustrate the total cost of his purchase (n).

$$4c + 3d = n$$

1. How much did Alex spend on CDs?

_____

2. How much did he spend on DVDs?

_____

3. Solve the equation.

_____

Warm-Up 216

What's the Problem?

Work It Out

Alex and his mother bought 11 CDs and 13 DVDs to give as presents. Each CD cost $19 and each DVD cost $22. He wrote an equation to illustrate the total cost of their purchase (n).

$$11c + 13d = n$$

1. How much did Alex and his mother spend on CDs?

_____

2. How much did they spend on DVDs?

_____

3. Solve the equation.

_____

What's the Problem?

Work It Out

Lauren's mom is 23 years older than Lauren. Lauren's dad is 4 times Lauren's age. Lauren is 11 years old. Lauren made equations to determine her parents' ages.

$m = 11 + 23$

$d = 4 \times 11$

Solve the equations to determine Lauren's parents' ages.

_____

_____

What's the Problem?

Work It Out

Lauren's grandfather is 68 years old. He is 4 times as old as Lauren's brother. Her grandmother is 72, which is 8 times the age of Lauren's cousin. Lauren made equations to determine their ages.

$b \times 4 = 68$

$c \times 8 = 72$

1. **How old is Lauren's brother?**

   _____

2. **How old is Lauren's cousin?**

   _____

Warm-Up 219

What's the Problem?

Work It Out

Anthony asked his friends if they could solve this problem: "I have a number (n), which is greater than 1. It is the square of a prime number. It is also the square root of a number greater than 64 but less than 100. What is my number?"

1. What is the number *n*?

_____

2. What is the square of the number?

_____

3. What is the square root of the number?

_____

- -

Warm-Up 220

What's the Problem?

Work It Out

Carissa told Anthony, "I have a riddle for you. I have a number (n), which still equals *n* when it is squared and when you take the square root. What is my number?"

1. What is the number *n*?

_____

2. What is the square of the number?

_____

3. What is the square root of the number?

_____

What's the Problem?

Work It Out

Natalia asked her friends this riddle: "What integer plus itself creates a sum that is the square root of a number greater than 60 and less than 100?"

Solve the riddle. (Start with a number and work up or down.)

• •

Warm-Up 222

What's the Problem?

Work It Out

Natalie's friend asked her to solve this riddle: "This number is the square root of a number greater than 100 but less than 200. It is an even number. It is not the square root of 144."

Solve the riddle. (Start with a number and work up or down.)

Algebra: solving equations

What's the Problem? Work It Out

Sal told Mary, "You can tell the age of my cat by evaluating this expression: 8(n) – 13 for n = 3 months."

Evaluate the expression. How old is Sal's cat?

_____

What's the Problem? Work It Out

Mary told Sal, "You can tell the age of my dog by evaluating the expression: 16p – 15 for p = 4 months."

Evaluate the expression. How old is Mary's dog?

_____

What's the Problem?

Stacy computed her sister's age using this equation with *n* as her sister's age.

$$(55 \div 11) - 4 + 22 = n + 3$$

Solve the equation. How old is her sister?

_____

· ·

What's the Problem?

Stacy computed her father's age using this equation with *n* as her father's age.

$$(9 \times 8) \div 12 + 48 - 11 = n + 3$$

Solve the equation. How old is her father?

_____

Warm-Up 227

What's the Problem?

Work It Out

Miguel passed out flyers at a county fair. How much he was paid was determined by a formula where a = 100, b = 20, and c = 12.

1. **Evaluate this expression to determine his pay in cents on the first day of the fair.**

   a/b + c

   _____

2. **Evaluate this expression to determine his pay in cents on the second day.**

   a(c) – b

   _____

- -

Warm-Up 228

What's the Problem?

Work It Out

1. **Evaluate this expression to determine Miguel's pay in cents on the third day.**

   (b)c + a(c)

   _____

2. **Evaluate this expression to determine his pay in cents on the fourth day.**

   ac + ab + cb + 28

   _____

Warm-Up 229

What's the Problem?

Work It Out

Christian told Ellen, "The function table here shows how much fuel I need to power my motorized bike over a long trip." Ellen replied back saying, "You forgot to finish the table."

Complete the function table for Christian.

Fuel (cups)	Distance It Can Travel
1	3 miles
2	6 miles
3	
4	
5	
6	
7	
8	

- -

Warm-Up 230

What's the Problem?

Work It Out

Ellen told Christian, "I am using a special motorbike fuel that I designed myself. The function table shows how much fuel I need to power my motorbike. I think my fuel works better and my bike feels lighter."

Complete the function table for Ellen.

Fuel (cups)	Distance It Can Travel
1	4.5 miles
2	
3	13.5 miles
4	
5	
6	
7	
8	

What's the Problem?   Work It Out

Jamie had $10 saved in a sock in his dresser. His aunt gave him $15 for his birthday. He spent $19 on a soccer ball. Jamie earned $7 for doing the dishes and spent $11 on a CD. He gave $2 to his little sister for watching the dog, and he found $4.50 in change on the street. This is the equation he wrote to show his gains and losses.

$$10 + 15 - 19 + 7 - 11 - 2 + 4.5 = n$$

Solve the equation to find out how much money Jamie now has.

_____

What's the Problem?   Work It Out

This expression represents the marbles Jamie won and lost in a marble tournament.

$$(-7) + (+ 4) + (-17) + (-3) + (+9) - (-13)$$

Solve the expression to determine how many marbles Jamie lost.

_____

What's the Problem?

Work It Out

Ruby has to pay a fine at home every time she makes her sister cry. She gets a bonus every time she helps her sister with her homework or reads to her. Ruby keeps a record of her fines (f) and her bonus payments (b). A fine costs her 9 cents. A bonus gives her 25 cents. The expression below represents her fines and bonuses for 1 week.

$11(-f) + 8b$

1. **Evaluate the expression.**

   _____

2. **At the end of the week, had Ruby earned or lost money? How much?**

   _____

· ·

Warm-Up
234

What's the Problem?

Work It Out

Ruby's second week was represented by this expression: $17(-f) + 11b$. Her third week was better: $9(-f) + 12b$.

1. **Evaluate the expression to find out if Ruby earned or lost money in the second week.**

   _____

2. **Do the same for the third week.**

   _____

Warm-Up 235

What's the Problem?   **Work It Out**

Javier wrote this sequence for his friend, Carla, and asked her to find the missing numbers.

(-1, -1, -2, _____, -5, -8, _____, -21, _____, -55, -89, _____, _____)

1. What numbers should Carla have found?

_____

2. What was Javier's pattern?

_____

Warm-Up 236

What's the Problem?   **Work It Out**

Carla asked Javier to solve her sequence and find the missing numbers.

(-144, -233, -377, _____, -987, _____, _____)

What numbers should Javier have found?

_____

What's the Problem?   Work It Out

April keeps her coins separated by type in different cups. She has 23 dimes, 44 nickels, and 51 quarters. She wrote the expression as 23d + 44n + 51q.

Evaluate the expression. How much money does she have in coins?

_____

What's the Problem?   Work It Out

April keeps her paper money in separate envelopes. She has 23 one-dollar bills in one envelope. She has 5 five-dollar bills in a second envelope. She has 4 ten-dollar bills in a third envelope. She wrote the expression 23d + 5f + 4t to express her total.

Evaluate the expression. How much money does she have in bills?

_____

What's the Problem?   Work It Out

Eleanor exclaimed, "I can't believe I overspent! Last week, I had $188 in my checking account, and today I have -$18 because I bought a cheerleading outfit and fancy shoes. I guess I thought I had more money in that account when I wrote the check."

How much money did Eleanor spend in all?

_____

What's the Problem?   Work It Out

Kimberly told Eleanor about a time when she overspent: "I thought I had over $100 in my checking account on Saturday. I bought a pair of skates, an outfit to go with it, and went to a skating movie that day. It turns out that I only had $73 because afterwards my account had -$16."

How much money did Kimberly spend altogether on Saturday?

_____

What's the Problem?

Work It Out

Clinton helped at a concession stand collecting tickets at the school fair. He kept a running account of the tickets he collected and gave out during the first hour.

5 + (-4) + (-9) + (+21) + (-7) + (+6) + (-6)

Evaluate the expression to determine how many tickets he had at the end of the first hour.

_____

What's the Problem?

Work It Out

Clinton found the afternoon at the school fair more hectic than the morning. He kept a running account of the tickets he collected and gave out in the afternoon.

(3 x 5) + 6 + (8 x 4) − 12 ÷ (2 x 3) + 2 + 7 − (6 x 3) + 4

1. **Evaluate the expression.**

   _____

2. **If each ticket is worth a quarter, how much money did Clinton collect in the afternoon?**

   _____

Warm-Up 243

What's the Problem?

Work It Out

Sherrie computed the size of her sticker collection using algebra. She counted the number of stickers on each page and recorded this expression.

$$8^2 + 3 + 9^2 + 4^2 + 13 + 4^2 + 8$$

Evaluate the expression. How many stickers does she have altogether?

_____

• •

Warm-Up 244

What's the Problem?

Work It Out

Sherrie found her father's collection of old baseball cards in envelopes that were stored inside an old trunk. She counted the contents of each envelope and recorded the number of baseball cards with this expression.

$$3^2 + 5^2 + 7^2 + 4 + 3^2 + 2 + 6^2 + 5 + 8$$

Evaluate the expression. How many baseball cards had her father saved?

_____

What's the Problem?

Work It Out

Julie went to the store to buy apples for herself and 5 friends. Each girl wanted one green apple. The apples were on sale for $0.67 each. Julie paid for the fruit with a $10-bill.

1. **If *y* represents the money Julie received in change, write an equation to find the value of *y*.**

   _____

2. **Solve the equation. How much money did Julie receive in change?**

   _____

What's the Problem?

Work It Out

While at the store, Julie bought 6 boxes of candy.
There were 12 candies in each box.
Julie opened 1 box and ate 4 candies.

1. **If *n* represents the total number of candies Julie has left, write an equation to find the value of *n*.**

   _____

2. **Solve the equation. How many candies does Julie still have?**

   _____

What's the Problem?

Work It Out

Cynthia was studying an equation that read:

$$2y + 4k + 3m - 2k + 5m - y = n$$

In order to simplify the equation, she needed to combine like terms.

1. Combine the like terms.

_____

2. Evaluate the equation for y = 1, k = 2, and m = 3.

_____

What's the Problem?

Work It Out

For extra credit, Cynthia volunteered to do a math problem in front of her class. When she walked to the front of the room, the board read:

$$4m + 7y - 3k + 6k - 1m - 6y = n$$

1. Help Cynthia simplify this equation.

_____

2. Evaluate the equation for y = 1, k = 2, and m = 3.

_____

Warm-Up 249

What's the Problem?

Work It Out

Marina put the stamps on her mother's mail when she mailed packets for her business. She started a function to help her figure out how many stamps to use for each package. Each stamp cost $0.44 for each ounce being mailed.

1. **Complete the function table for Marina.**

2. **How much would it cost to mail an 11-ounce package?**

   _____

3. **How much would it cost to mail a 12-ounce package?**

   _____

Ounces	Cost
1	$0.44
2	$0.88
3	$1.32
4	$1.76
5	
6	
7	
8	
9	
10	

Warm-Up 250

What's the Problem?

Work It Out

When Marina heard the cost of postage was going up to $0.47 an ounce, she knew that she would need a new function for mailing packages.

1. **Create a table or function for stamps at the $0.47 per ounce cost.**

2. **How much would it cost to mail a 5-ounce package?**

   _____

3. **How much would it cost to mail a 9-ounce package?**

   _____

4. **How much would a 12-ounce package cost to mail?**

   _____

Ounces	Cost

ANSWER KEY

Warm-Up 1

Numbers between 15 and 50: 15, 16, 17, 18, 19, 20, 21, 22, 23, 24, 25, 26, 27, 28, 29, 30, 31, 32, 33, 34, 35, 36, 37, 38, 39, 40, 41, 42, 43, 44, 45, 46, 47, 48, 49, 50

Digits that equal 10: 19, 28, 37, 46

Jamie earned 40¢. (10¢ x 4 = 40¢)

Pattern: As first digit increases, second digit decreases (so 55, 64, 73, 82, and 91 would be the next numbers if continuing)

Warm-Up 2

Palindromes between 10 and 100:
11, 22, 33, 44, 55, 66, 77, 88, 99 (9 total)

Jessica collected $2.25. (25¢ x 9 = $2.25)

Palindromes between 100 and 200:
101, 111, 121, 131, 141, 151, 161, 171, 181, 191 (10 total)

Warm-Up 3

1. 1 is not a possible football score.

2. 1 Touchdown, 1 Field Goal, 1 Point After Touchdown (6 + 3 + 1)

   1 Touchdown, 2 Safeties (6 + 2 + 2)

   2 Field Goals, 2 Safeties (3 + 3 + 2 + 2)

   5 Safeties (2 + 2 + 2 + 2 + 2)

3. 1 Touchdown (6)

   2 Field Goals (3 + 3)

   3 Safeties (2 + 2 + 2)

4. 1, 2, 3, 4, 5, 8, 9

Warm-Up 4

There are 4 possible combinations.

3-pound bags	5-pound bags	Total Weight
9 (27)	8 (40)	67 pounds
19 (57)	2 (10)	67 pounds
4 (12)	11 (55)	67 pounds
14 (42)	5 (25)	67 pounds

- First list the multiples of 3 that end in 7 because a 7 in the ones place is needed for a total of 67 pounds (9 x 3 = 27 and 19 x 3 = 57). Then take the total amount of needed flour (67 pounds) and subtract the above values to see what combination of 5 is needed. (67 − 27 = 40, so 8 of the 5-pound bags are needed. 67 − 57 = 10, so 2 of the 5-pound bags are needed.)

- Then list the multiples of 3 that end in 2 and the multiples of 5 that end in 5 so that when the values are added together, there is a 7 in the ones place for a total of 67 pounds.

Warm-Up 5

Mark can arrange the trophies in 24 different ways.

SFBT	FSBT	TFSB	BFTS
SFTB	FSTB	TFBS	BFST
SBFT	FBST	TBSF	BTFS
SBTF	FBTS	TBFS	BTSF
STBF	FTSB	TSBF	BSTF
STFB	FTBS	TSFB	BSFT

Warm-Up 6

Laurie can make 30 different outfit combinations.

Blouses	Bottoms	Blouses	Bottoms
red	black	red	striped
blue	black	blue	striped
pink	black	pink	striped
purple	black	purple	striped
yellow	black	yellow	striped
orange	black	orange	striped
red	brown	red	jeans
blue	brown	blue	jeans
pink	brown	pink	jeans
purple	brown	purple	jeans
yellow	brown	yellow	jeans
orange	brown	orange	jeans
red	white		
blue	white		
pink	white		
purple	white		
yellow	white		
orange	white		

Warm-Up 7

Jeanette can make 32 different outfit combinations.

Blouses	Bottoms	Hats	Blouses	Bottoms	Hats
green	blue	beret	green	blue	cap
pink	blue	beret	pink	blue	cap
red	blue	beret	red	blue	cap
blue	blue	beret	blue	blue	cap
green	black	beret	green	black	cap
pink	black	beret	pink	black	cap
red	black	beret	red	black	cap
blue	black	beret	blue	black	cap
green	striped	beret	green	striped	cap
pink	striped	beret	pink	striped	cap
red	striped	beret	red	striped	cap
blue	striped	beret	blue	striped	cap
green	white	beret	green	white	cap
pink	white	beret	pink	white	cap
red	white	beret	red	white	cap
blue	white	beret	blue	white	cap

Warm-Up 8

There are 27 possible combinations. There are enough numbers to go around, with 9 numbers remaining.

333	433	533
334	434	534
335	435	535
343	443	543
344	444	544
345	445	545
353	453	553
354	454	554
355	455	555

Warm-Up 9

It took 15 days to travel 3,375 miles.

Day	Miles Traveled	Running Total
1	50	50
2	75	125
3	100	225
4	125	350
5	150	500
6	175	675
7	200	875
8	225	1,100
9	250	1,350
10	275	1,625
11	300	1,925
12	325	2,250
13	350	2,600
14	375	2,975
15	400	3,375

Warm-Up 10

There are 64 possible combinations. There are 6 possible combinations equaling 5 (shown in bold).

1, 1, 1	2, 1, 1	**3, 1, 1**	4, 1, 1
1, 1, 2	**2, 1, 2**	3, 1, 2	4, 1, 2
1, 1, 3	2, 1, 3	3, 1, 3	4, 1, 3
1, 1, 4	2, 1, 4	3, 1, 4	4, 1, 4
1, 2, 1	**2, 2, 1**	3, 2, 1	4, 2, 1
1, 2, 2	2, 2, 2	3, 2, 2	4, 2, 2
1, 2, 3	2, 2, 3	3, 2, 3	4, 2, 3
1, 2, 4	2, 2, 4	3, 2, 4	4, 2, 4
1, 3, 1	2, 3, 1	3, 3, 1	4, 3, 1
1, 3, 2	2, 3, 2	3, 3, 2	4, 3, 2
1, 3, 3	2, 3, 3	3, 3, 3	4, 3, 3
1, 3, 4	2, 3, 4	3, 3, 4	4, 3, 4
1, 4, 1	2, 4, 1	3, 4, 1	4, 4, 1
1, 4, 2	2, 4, 2	3, 4, 2	4, 4, 2
1, 4, 3	2, 4, 3	3, 4, 3	4, 4, 3
1, 4, 4	2, 4, 4	3, 4, 4	4, 4, 4

Warm-Up 11

Start guessing with quarters or nickels. Because there was $0.35 involved, you could guess either 7 nickels or 2 nickels with a combination of quarters that ends in $0.25. There couldn't be too many half dollars in 20 rounds with only about $4.00, so guess 2, 3, or 4 half dollars.

Sample Guesses:

Quarters	Nickels	Half Dollars	Total
11 ($2.75)	8 ($0.40)	1 ($0.50)	$3.65 (too little)
12 ($3.00)	6 ($0.30)	2 ($1.00)	$4.30 (too little)
13 ($3.25)	2 ($0.10)	5 ($2.50)	$5.85 (too much)
10 ($2.50)	**7 ($0.35)**	**3 ($1.50)**	**$4.35 (Correct Answer)**

Warm-Up 12

Mark spent about $50 for only 3 items.
Try 1 higher-priced and 2 lesser-priced items.
Keep adding 3 prices until you come up with a total of $49.95.

Sample Guess 1: $29.50 + $19.75 + $7.50 = $56.75
(too much)

Sample Guess 2: $19.75 + $15.75 + $12.95 = $48.45
(too little)

Correct Answer: $29.50 + $12.95 + $7.50 = $49.95

Mark bought a baseball glove, a bat, and sunglasses.

Warm-Up 13

Guess what 4 items would equal about $110. Try 1 higher-priced and 3 lesser-priced items. Keep adding four prices until you come up with a total of $108.45.

Sample Guess 1: $59.75 + $19.95 + $15.25 + $11.25 = $106.20 (too little)

Sample Guess 2: $49.50 + $19.95 + $13.50 + $15.25 = $98.20 (way too little)

Correct Answer:
$59.75 + $19.95 + $13.50 + $15.25 = $108.45

Jasmine bought running shoes, a juniors' jacket, warm-up sweats, and hair scarves.

Warm-Up 14

Total $1.48 in 19 coins

Sample Guesses:

Pennies	Nickels	Dimes	Quarters	Total
8 (.08)	2 (.10)	6 (.60)	3 (.75)	$1.53 (too much)
8 (.08)	1 (.05)	7 (.70)	3 (.75)	$1.58 (too much)
3 (.03)	**6 (.30)**	**9 (.90)**	**1 (.25)**	**$1.48 (Correct Answer)**

Warm-Up 15

Start with any small number for Day 1, and then add 6 more to each following day. The total for 7 days must be 182.

Sample Guesses:

Day 1	Day 2	Day 3	Day 4	Day 5	Day 6	Day 7
2	8	14	20	26	32	38 = 140 (too little)
6	12	18	24	30	36	42 = 168 (too little)
8	**14**	**20**	**26**	**32**	**38**	**44 = 182 (Correct Answer)**

Warm-Up 16

Four brothers together weigh 600 pounds.
Lenny = 2 x Larry
Lenny = Lyndon ÷ 2
Lionel = Larry

Sample Guess 1:
Larry = 100 pounds
Lionel = 100 pounds (Larry's twin)
Lenny = 200 pounds (twice as much as Larry)
Lyndon = 400 pounds (twice Lenny's weight)
Total 800 pounds (too much)

Sample Guess 2:
Larry = 75 pounds
Lionel = 75 pounds (Larry's twin)
Lenny = 150 pounds (twice as much as Larry)
Lyndon = 300 pounds (twice Lenny's weight)
Total 600 pounds (Correct Answer)

Warm-Up 17

Need 11 books totaling $41.75.
Two book prices, $2.95 and $4.50.

Sample Guess 1: 4 at $2.95 and 7 at $4.50
$11.80 + $31.50 = $43.30 (too much)

Sample Guess 2: 6 at $2.95 and 5 at $4.50
$17.70 + $22.50 = $40.20 (too little)

Sample Guess 3: 5 at $2.95 and 6 at $4.50
$14.75 + $27.00 = $41.75 (Correct Answer)

Warm-Up 18

Total spent is $79.30.
Sample Guess 1:
2 face masks $9.50 each = $19.00
2 beanies at $7.95 each = $15.90
3 pairs of gloves at $12.15 each = $36.45
Total = $71.35 (too little)

Sample Guess 2:
3 face masks $9.50 each = $28.50
2 beanies at $7.95 each = $15.90
3 pairs of gloves at $12.15 each = $36.45
Total = $80.85 (too much)

Sample Guess 3:
2 face masks at $9.50 each = $19.00
3 beanies at $7.95 each = $23.85
3 pairs of gloves at $12.15 each = $36.45
Total = $79.30 (Correct Answer)

Warm-Up 19

44 points on 21 shots; three 1-point shots is given

Sample Guesses:

1-point	2-point	3-point	Total
3 (3)	10 (20)	8 (24)	47 (too high)
3 (3)	8 (16)	10 (30)	49 (too high)
3 (3)	12 (24)	6 (18)	45 (too high)
3 (3)	14 (28)	4 (12)	43 (too low)
3 (3)	**13 (26)**	**5 (15)**	**44 (Correct Answer)**

Warm-Up 20

Sample Guesses:

Face Cards (10)	Number Cards (4)
5 (50)	4 (16) = 9 cards/66 points (too high)
4 (40)	**5 (20) = 9 cards/60 points (Correct Answer)**

Warm-Up 21

Train Stops	Pass. Boarding
1st	1
2nd	4
3rd	10
4th	22
5th	46
6th	94
7th	190
8th	382
9th	**766**

Pattern = (n x 2) + 2, where *n* is the previous number of passengers boarding, for example (22 x 2) + 2 = 46

Another pattern is where you double the difference between the previous 2 numbers of passengers boarding.

1,515 total passengers boarded the train during the 9 stops.

Warm-Up 22

194 + 59 = 253 total passengers on the train

Train Stops	Pass. Who Left	Remaining Pass.
1st	9	244
2nd	17	227
3rd	33	194
4th	65	129
5th	**129**	**0**

The train made 5 stops. 129 passengers left at the last stop.

Pattern = (n x 2) − 1, where *n* is the previous number of passengers who left, for example (9 x 2) − 1 = 17

Warm-Up 23

Day	Laps
1	1
2	2
3	4
4	7
5	11
6	16
7	22
8	**29**

Jill swam 29 laps on the 8th day.

The pattern is to increase by 1 more lap each day (+1, +2, +3, +4, etc.).

Warm-Up 24

Child	Silver Dollars
1st	1
2nd	1
3rd	2
4th	3
5th	5
6th	8
7th	**13**
8th	**21**
9th	**34**
10th	**55**

Caleb got 55 silver dollars. (This is the Fibonacci sequence.)

Pattern = Add the 2 preceding numbers: 1 + 2 = 3, 2 + 3 = 5, etc.

Warm-Up 25

Week	Chicks
1st	2
2nd	7
3rd	17
4th	**37**
5th	**77**
6th	**157**
7th	317

Pattern = (n x 2) + 3, where *n* is the number of chicks, for example (2 x 2) + 3 = 7

Another pattern is that the rate of chicks hatching each week doubles the next week: +5, +10, +20, +40, etc.

Warm-Up 26

Lemons	Cents	Lemons	Cents
1st	1	9th	45
2nd	3	**10th**	**55**
3rd	6	11th	66
4th	10	12th	78
5th	15	13th	91
6th	21	14th	105
7th	28	**15th**	**120**
8th	36		

Marty will earn 55 cents for the 10th lemon and $1.20 for the 15th lemon.

Pattern = +2, +3, +4, +5, etc.

Warm-Up 27

Chapter	Page #
1	1
2	4
3	9
4	16
5	25
6	36
7	49
8	64

Pattern = +3, +5, +7, +9, +11, +13, etc.

or

Pattern = Chapter^2

Warm-Up 28

(17, 26, 37, **50**, **65**, **82**, 101, 122, 145)

Page 65 has the magic spell.

Pattern = +9, +11, +13, +15, +17, etc.

Warm-Up 29

Hour	Flies	Hour	Flies
1st	2	8th	256
2nd	4	9th	512
3rd	8	10th	1,024
4th	16	11th	2,048
5th	32	12th	4,096
6th	64	**13th**	**8,192**
7th	128		

There will be 8,192 flies at the 13th hour.

Pattern = (n x 2) where *n* is the previous number of fruit flies

Warm-Up 30

Week	Bags
1st	80
2nd	40
3rd	20
4th	**10**
5th	**5**
6th	**2.5**
7th	**1.25**

They will collect 10, 5, 2.5, and 1.25 over the next 4 weeks.

Pattern = (n ÷ 2), where *n* is the previous number of bags

Warm-Up 31

There are 8 possible outcomes.

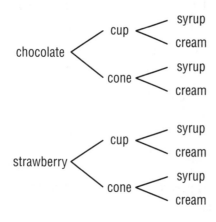

Warm-Up 32

There are 8 possible outcomes (4 combinations for each coin).

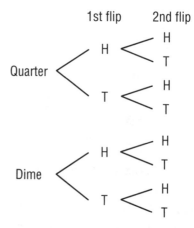

Warm-Up 33

There are 24 possible arrangements.

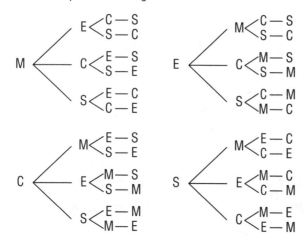

Warm-Up 34

There are 6 possible seating arrangements.

R < J
      C

J < R
      C

C < R
      J

Warm-Up 35

There are 24 possible arrangements.

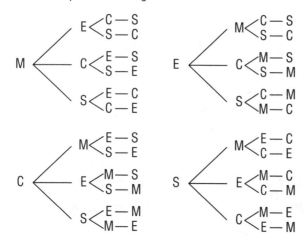

Warm-Up 36

There are 27 possible outcomes. The probability of spinning a 3 each time is 1 in 27.

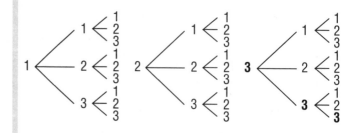

Warm-Up 37

There are 16 possible outcomes (8 combinations for each coin).

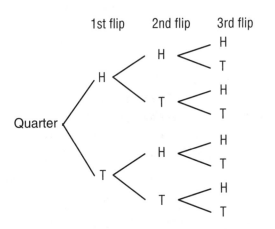

Warm-Up 38

There are 27 possible outcomes.

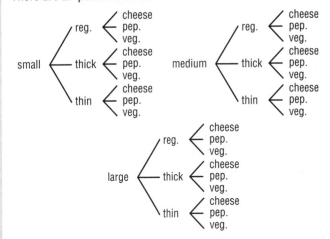

Warm-Up 39

There are 64 possible outcomes (16 for each number on the die). A tree diagram for first rolling a 1 is shown below. The tree diagrams for first rolling a 2, 3, or 4 would look the same.

Warm-Up 40

There are 6 possible outcomes.

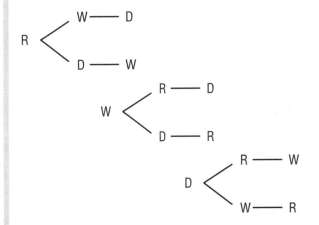

Warm-Up 41

Jill = 16 + Reggie

Jonathan = Reggie − 17

Anne = 15 + Jill

Joseph = 11 + Jonathan

Jonathan = 18

Jonathan = **18** x 13¢ = **$2.34**

Joseph = 11 + 18 = **29** x 13¢ = **$3.77**

Reggie = 18 + 17 = **35** x 13¢ = **$4.55**

Jill = 16 + 35 = **51** x 13¢ = **$6.63**

Anne = 15 + 51 = **66** x 13¢ = **$8.58**

Warm-Up 42

potatoes = 3 x turnips

corn = 2 x potatoes

tomatoes + beets = 11

beets = 5

potatoes = 4 x tomatoes

11 − 5 = **6 tomatoes**

4 x 6 = **24 potatoes**

2 x 24 = **48 corn**

24 ÷ 3 = **8 turnips**

5 beets

Warm-Up 43

Joe = 6 + Mike
Art = 4 + Joe
Jimmy = 8 + Joe
Steve = 16
Steve = Jimmy − 1

Steve's ball = **16 bounces**
Jimmy's ball = 16 + 1 = **17 bounces**
Joe's ball = 17 − 8 = **9 bounces**
Art's ball = 4 + 9 = **13 bounces**
Mike's ball = 9 − 6 = **3 bounces**

Warm-Up 44

Roman = 2 x Ricky
Roland = Ricky ÷ 2
Roger = 32
Grandfather = 2 x Roger
Roman = Grandfather ÷ 2

Roger's fish = **32 ounces**
Grandfather's fish = 2 x 32 = **64 ounces**
Roman's fish = 64 ÷ 2 = **32 ounces**
Ricky's fish = 32 ÷ 2 = **16 ounces**
Roland's fish = 16 ÷ 2 = **8 ounces**

Warm-Up 45

Shane = 6 + Monica
Monica + Minnie = 17
Joey = Shane − 8
Minnie = 5
Erica = Shane + 1

Minnie = **5 marbles**
Monica = 17 − 5 = **12 marbles**
Shane = 6 + 12 = **18 marbles**
Joey = 18 − 8 = **10 marbles**
Erica = 18 +1 = **19 marbles (most)**

Warm-Up 46

gave away 10 fish to 4 friends = 40 fish

37 baby fish hatched

7 fish died

88 fish left at week's end

88 + 40 − 37 + 7 = 98 fish at the beginning of the week

Warm-Up 47

Amy = 2 x Alana
Amy = Allison ÷ 2
Anthony = 2 x Allison
Anthony = Ashton ÷ 2
Arto = 4
Arto = Alana ÷ 2

Arto = **4 minutes**
Alana = 4 x 2 = **8 minutes**
Amy = 2 x 8 = **16 minutes**
Allison = 2 x 16 = **32 minutes**
Anthony = 2 x 32 = **64 minutes** (1 hour 4 minutes)
Ashton = 2 x 64 = **128 minutes** (2 hours 8 minutes)

Warm-Up 48

- Albert's favorite planet is farther than the distance from Earth to the sun. That eliminates Mercury, Venus, and Earth because of the distances.

- It is farther from Pluto than it is from Earth. That eliminates Neptune and Pluto.

- It is farther from the sun than the combined distances of Jupiter and Saturn from the sun. That eliminates Jupiter and Saturn.

- Only Uranus fits all of the criteria.

Warm-Up 49

length = 3 x width
height = length ÷ 2
width = 2 x lizard length
lizard = 10 inches long

width = 2 x 10 = **20 inches**
length = 3 x 20 = **60 inches**
height = 60 ÷ 2 = **30 inches**

Volume = length x width x height
Volume = 60 x 20 x 30 = **36,000 cubic inches**

Warm-Up 50

Katy = 10
Katrina = 3 x Caroline
Carmen = 3 + Katrina
Kristin = Carmen + 5
Caroline = Katy ÷ 2

Katy = **10 years old**
Caroline = 10 ÷ 2 = **5 years old**
Katrina = 3 x 5 = **15 years old**
Carmen = 3 + 15 = **18 years old**
Kristin = 18 + 5 = **23 years old**

Warm-Up 51
1. 2, 3, 4, 6, 8, 9
2. none
3. 3, 7, 9

Warm-Up 52
1. 7
2. none
3. 3, 9

Warm-Up 53
1. 100   4. 70
2. 5   5. 8
3. 30   6. 7

Warm-Up 54
1. 9   4. 5
2. 9   5. 2,000
3. 7   6. 5,000

Warm-Up 55
$260.08

Warm-Up 56
$1,241.70

Warm-Up 57
1. 6 lbs.
2. 1/10 lb.
3. 1/10 lb.

Warm-Up 58
1. 3 3/4 yards
2. 5/8 yard

Warm-Up 59
1. $32.40   3. $40.50
2. $8.10   4. 45

Warm-Up 60
1. $20.25
2. no
3. $23.54
4. $37.74

Warm-Up 61
1. 89
2. 85.7 or 86
3. 92.3 or 92

Warm-Up 62
1. 90.6 or 91
2. 78
3. 70

Warm-Up 63
1. 122
2. 9,638
3. Answers may vary.
   10-year-old = 1,220

Warm-Up 64
1. 30,000,000
2. 720,000,000
3. 8,333

Warm-Up 65
1. 55.8 lbs.
2. 15.3 lbs.
3. 13.5 lbs.
4. 5.4 lbs. (6%)

Warm-Up 66
Jeffrey
   w = 88.66 lbs.
   p = 24.31 lbs.
   f = 21.45 lbs.
Teresa
   w = 62 lbs.
   p = 17 lbs.
   f = 15 lbs.
Hazel
   w = 42.16 lbs.
   p = 11.56 lbs
   f = 10.2 lbs.
Jonathan
   w = 69.44 lbs.
   p = 19.04 lbs.
   f = 16.8 lbs.

Warm-Up 67
country = 302,000,000
state = 37,000,000
city = 4,000,000

Warm-Up 68
1. NY = 19,000,000
   CA = 37,000,000
   HI = 1,000,000
   TX = 24,000,000
   MI = 10,000,000
   WV = 2,000,000
   MT = 1,000,000
   NV = 3,000,000
   MN = 5,000,000
   OH = 11,000,000
2. California
3. Montana
4. They provide an easy-to-see
   approximation that makes them
   quicker to compare.

Warm-Up 69
Jefferson = 83
Adams = 90 (He didn't reach his
   birthday in 1826.)
Monroe = 73

Warm-Up 70
Carson = 57
Curie = 67
Bell = 75
Costeau = 87
Edison = 84
Einstein = 76

Warm-Up 71
1. $40   4. $5
2. $20   5. $2.50
3. $10

Warm-Up 72
1. $40   4. $10; $7
2. $25   5. $10 (10%)
3. $8

Warm-Up 73
1. Janet = 4
   Jennifer = 8
   Julia = 6
   Justine = 3
2. 3
3. 1/8

Warm-Up 74
1. 3/4
2. 1/4

Warm-Up 75
house = 2,400 sq. ft.
garage = 1,600 sq. ft.
lawn = 2,000 sq. ft.
driveway = 800 sq. ft.
gardens = 640 sq. ft.
sidewalk = 560 sq. ft.

Warm-Up 76
1. driveway, gardens, sidewalk
2. house, garage
3. driveway, gardens, sidewalk,
   lawn

Warm-Up 77
1. 25
2. The others are prime numbers
   with only themselves and 1 as
   factors.

Warm-Up 78
1. 72 (12 factors)
2. 9 (3 factors)

Warm-Up 79
1. $439.50
2. $377.96

Warm-Up 80
1. $188.98
2. $9.45

Warm-Up 81
48

Warm-Up 82
96

Warm-Up 83
1. 2
2. 2, 3, 5, 7, 11, 13, 17, 19, 23, 29,
   31, 37, 41, 43, 47, 53, 59, 61,
   67, 71, 73, 79, 83, 89, 97

Warm-Up 84

No. 999 is composite because it is divisible by 3, 9, and other numbers. The largest prime number under 1,000 is 997.

Warm-Up 85

1. Yes, 89.6 rounds to 90.
2. 91.857 rounds to 92.

Warm-Up 86

1. 3.142   3. 3.1
2. 3.14   4. 3

Warm-Up 87

1. Possible mental addition = 37
2. 36.2

Warm-Up 88

1. Possible mental addition = $45
2. $45.06

Warm-Up 89

1. $338.49
2. $67.70
3. $270.79

Warm-Up 90

1. $24.37
2. $295.16
3. $4.84

Warm-Up 91

equil. triangle: P = 6 cm, 4 eq. tri.
rhombus: P = 4 cm; 2 eq. tri.
regular trapezoid: P = 5 cm; 3 eq. tri.
parallelogram: P = 6 cm; 4 eq. tri.

Warm-Up 92

1. ▱ ▨ ▦

2. ▱

Warm-Up 93

# of Squares	Perimeter
1	4 cm
2	6 cm
3	8 cm
4	10 cm
5	12 cm
6	14 cm
7	16 cm
8	18 cm

Warm-Up 94

1. 18 cm
2. 24 cm; 30 cm

Warm-Up 95

1. 6 O   6. 2 A, 2 O
2. 3 A   7. 2 A, 2 O
3. 2 A, 1 R   8. 5 O
4. 4 R   9. 1 O, 2 A
5. 4 R   10. 8 O

Warm-Up 96

1. 9 cm   6. 9 cm
2. 9 cm   7. 8 cm
3. 9.5 cm   8. 7.5 cm
4. 8 cm   9. 8.5 cm
5. 10 cm   10. 8 cm

Warm-Up 97

triangle: s = 3, v = 3, d = 0
square: s = 4, v = 4, d = 2
pentagon: s = 5, v = 5, d = 5
hexagon: s = 6, v = 6, d = 9
octagon: s = 8, v = 8, d = 20

Warm-Up 98

decagon: s = 10, v = 10, d = 35

Warm-Up 99

Hexagons	Perimeter
1	6 cm
2	10 cm
3	14 cm
4	18 cm
5	22 cm

Warm-Up 100

1. pattern =
   (number of hexagons x 4) + 2
2. 26 cm
3. 42 cm

Warm-Up 101

Each equilateral triangle has 60 degrees in each angle.

Warm-Up 102

Each isosceles right triangle has one 90-degree angle and two 45-degree angles.

Warm-Up 103

1. 24 sq. ft.
2. 24 wooden pieces

Warm-Up 104

1. 18 sq. ft.
2. 12 sq. ft.

Warm-Up 105

1. 16 in.
2. 16 in.
3. 256 sq. in.
4. 64 in.

Warm-Up 106

1. 24 cm
2. 24 cm
3. 576 cm sq.
4. 96 cm

Warm-Up 107

1. 80 sq. ft.
2. 81 sq. ft.
3. Catherine's room is larger by 1 square foot.

Warm-Up 108

1. Catherine's closet = 32 sq. ft.
   Kevin's closet = 27 sq. ft.
2. Catherine's closet is bigger.

Warm-Up 109

1. 360 cubic inches
2. 60 friends can be served

Warm-Up 110

1. 576 cubic inches
2. 96 friends can be served

Warm-Up 111

1. 11,520 cubic feet
2. 384 cubic feet

Warm-Up 112

1. 180,000 cubic feet
2. 180,000 cubic feet of air
3. 600 cubic feet of air per person

Warm-Up 113

1. quadrant 4
2. 90-degree angles
3. angles 1 and 3
4. angle 1
5. 360 degrees

Warm-Up 114

1. quadrant 1
2. Angles that equal 180°:
   1 and 2
   2 and 3
   3 and 4
   4 and 1
3. angles 1 and 3
4. angle 2

Warm-Up 115

1. perpendicular
2. parallel
3. intersecting, but not perpendicular
4. skew

Warm-Up 116

Angle A = 150 degrees
Angle B = 30 degrees
Angle C = 150 degrees

Warm-Up 117

1. 18 feet
2. C. isosceles

Warm-Up 118

1. 16 sq. ft.
2. 8 sq. ft.

Warm-Up 119

1. C. right
2. equal in area

Warm-Up 120
1. 120 sq. ft.
2. $360

Warm-Up 121
regular trapezoid

Warm-Up 122
rhombus

Warm-Up 123
78.5 sq. ft.

Warm-Up 124
31.4 feet

Warm-Up 125
1. rectangular prism
2. 6 faces
3. 8 vertices
4. 12 edges

Warm-Up 126
1. triangular prism
2. 5 faces
3. 6 vertices
4. 9 edges

Warm-Up 127
1. 180 degrees
2. 90 degrees
3. 120 degrees
4. 60 degrees

Warm-Up 128
1. (1, 360)
   (2, 180)
   (3, 120)
   (4, 90)
   (5, 72)
   (6, 60)
   (8, 45)
   (9, 40)
   (10, 36)
   (12, 30)
   (15, 24)
   (18, 20)
2. There are 24 numbers (12 pairs) that divide evenly into 360.

Warm-Up 129
1. 2 min.
2. 6 min.
3. 12 min.
4. (3, 3)
5. (5, 5)

Warm-Up 130
1. (8, 8)
2. (2, 2)
3. (1, 8)
4. (9, 12)

Warm-Up 131
1. 30 cm
2. 90 cm

Warm-Up 132
small pencil eraser = cm
eyelash = cm
fingernail = cm
width of little finger = cm.
quarter = in.
thickness of a notebook = cm
thickness of a math book = in.
width of a pencil = cm
width of an ear = in.

Warm-Up 133
1. 124 ft.
2. 960 sq. ft.

Warm-Up 134
1. 122 ft.
2. 900 sq. ft.
3. Yes

Warm-Up 135
1. Sean's flight was longer at about 1,220.47 in. David's was 1,188 in.
2. 32.47 in.

Warm-Up 136
1. Sean's was farther at about 1,259.84 in. David's was 1,242 in.
2. 17.84 in.

Warm-Up 137
1. 3 miles
2. 12 miles

Warm-Up 138
4 miles per hour

Warm-Up 139
50 miles per hour

Warm-Up 140
350 miles per hour

Warm-Up 141
1. $10
2. $36
3. $360

Warm-Up 142
1. 52,800 feet
2. 17,600 yards
3. 25,000 footsteps

Warm-Up 143
1. 21,120 feet
2. 7,040 yards

Warm-Up 144
13 minutes per mile

Warm-Up 145
1. 106 days
2. 15 weeks and 1 day

Warm-Up 146
1. September = 30 days
   October = 31 days
   November = 30 days
   December = 31 days
   January = 31 days
   February = 28 days
   March = 31 days
   April = 30 days
   May = 31 days
   June = 30 days
   July = 31 days
   August = 31 days
2. 365 days
3. 290 days

Warm-Up 147
2 hours 46 minutes 40 seconds

Warm-Up 148
1. $100
2. 50 hours

Warm-Up 149
1. 8 oz.
2. 32 oz.
3. 128 oz.

Warm-Up 150
1. 32 oz.
2. 34 oz.
3. 94.1%

Warm-Up 151
1. 144
2. 36
3. 72
4. 12

Warm-Up 152
1. 9
2. 1,296

Warm-Up 153
Possible answers:
1 centimeter = width of your little finger
1 inch = length of a small paper clip
1 foot = a bit longer than a sheet of paper
1 yard = width of a front door
1 meter = height of a kindergartener
1 mile = distance a car travels in 5 minutes
1 gram = weight of a penny
1 ounce = weight of a slice of bread
1 pound = weight of a large potato
1 pint = a medium-sized drink
1 quart = a small container of milk
1 gallon = a container of gasoline

Warm-Up 154
Answers will vary.
Warm-Up 155
1. 2,000 ml
2. 2,000 eyedroppers
3. 2 liters
Warm-Up 156
1. 140 ml more
2. 500 ml
3. 360 ml
Warm-Up 157
1. 4 mph
2. 4 mph
Warm-Up 158
1. 50 mph
2. 66.7 or 67 mph
Warm-Up 159
500 ft. per min.
Warm-Up 160
4 mph
Warm-Up 161
1. 45°, acute
2. 120°, obtuse
3. 90°, right
4. 70°, acute
Warm-Up 162
Answers will vary.
Warm-Up 163
8:00 = 120°
1:00 = 30°
3:00 = 90°
6:30 = 15°
Warm-Up 164
Possible answers:
135° = 10:30
60° = 2:00
30° = 5:30
90° = 9:00
Warm-Up 165
Red to Total
9 to 30 or 3 to 10
9 : 30 or 3 : 10
9/30 or 3/10
0.3
30%
Brown to Total
12 to 30 or 2 to 5
12 : 30 or 2 : 5
12/30 or 2/5
0.4
40%

Warm-Up 166
Blue to Brown
6 to 12 or 1 to 2
6 : 12 or 1 : 2
6/12 or 1/2
0.5
50%
Orange to Brown
2 to 12 or 1 to 6
2 : 12 or 1 : 6
2/12 or 1/6
0.167 or 0.17
16.7% or 17%
Warm-Up 167
1. 12 : 28 or 3 : 7
   12/28 or 3/7
2. 12 : 16 or 3 : 4
   12/16 or 3/4
Warm-Up 168
1. 260 : 510 or 26 : 51
2. 260 : 250 or 26 : 25
Warm-Up 169
1. Angela = 2,250 ft.
   Ellen = 2,500 ft.
   Ricardo = 3,500 ft.
   Tommy = 2,750 ft.
   Linda = 3,750 ft.
2. Total = 14,750 ft.
Warm-Up 170
1. 1,238,500 ft.
2. 234.6 miles
3. 8.8 laps
Warm-Up 171
1. College A, $35 billion
2. College E
3. College E
4. College C
Warm-Up 172
Graph should show the following values:
Year 1: T = $14,000; R = $8,000
Year 2: T = $15,000; R = $8,500
Year 3: T = $16,000; R = $9,000
Year 4: T = $17,000; R = $9,500
Year 5: T = $18,000; R = $10,000
Warm-Up 173
1. tortoise
2. cat
3. horse
4. hippo
5. 70 years old
Warm-Up 174
1. Check bar graph for accuracy.
2. lions
3. 9

Warm-Up 175
1. 28 bones
2. 114 bones
3. 64 bones
4. 206 bones
Warm-Up 176
1. snow skiing; 1,000 calories in an hour
2. 300 calories
3. 450 calories
4. 1,950 calories
5. 1,100 calories
Warm-Up 177
1. the first test
2. 8 tests
3. 91% average
4. Linda's grades were low the first week and then were mostly in the 90 to 100 percent range.
Warm-Up 178
1. Linda's math grades vary with several poor grades, but generally increased in score.
2. The grades did improve for a time either because the work was easier or she studied harder.
3. The 10th test may have had more difficult math problems or Linda may not have studied enough for the test.
Warm-Up 179
A = gunship
B = aircraft carrier
C = submarine
D = destroyer
E = battleship
Warm-Up 180
Gunship = (4, 6)
Destroyer = (8, 5)
Submarine = (9, 3)
Aircraft carrier = (10, 8)
Battleship = (10, 0)
Warm-Up 181
1. The general trend was decreasing.
2. It was probably hotter that day.
3. difference = 14 mL loss
Warm-Up 182
Choice B; 7 days in 1 week, 7 values given in graph
Warm-Up 183
1. 55   4. 15
2. 4   5. 17
3. 1

Warm-Up 184
1. Check line plot for accuracy.
2. 20
3. 7
4. 64

Warm-Up 185
1. music videos; 56 votes
2. 16 votes
3. news and serious drama; 4 votes
4. Students prefer music, talent, and reality shows.

Warm-Up 186
Answers will vary.

Warm-Up 187
1. hamburgers
2. salad and chicken
3. hamburgers and pizza

Warm-Up 188
1.

2. 32 students
3. tacos
4. macaroni & cheese

Warm-Up 189
1. Generally, the puppy grew heavier each week.
2. 10 pounds
3. between weeks 5 and 7

Warm-Up 190
1. Check line graph for accuracy.
2. 10 in.
3. week 8

Warm-Up 191
1. 1/4 or 25%
2. 3/4 or 75%
3. 1/4 or 25%
4. 3/4 or 75%

Warm-Up 192
1. 1/8 or 12.5%
2. 6/8 or 3/4, or 75%
3. 7/8 or 87.5%
4. equal chance
5. 3/8 or 37.5%

Warm-Up 193
1. 1/10 or 10%
2. 9/10 or 90%
3. 2/16 or 1/8, or 12.5%
4. 14/16 or 7/8, or 87.5%

Warm-Up 194
1. 4/40 or 1/10, or 10%
2. 2/40 or 1/20, 5%
3. 36/40 or 9/10, or 90%
4. 38/40 or 19/20, or 95%
5. 6/40 or 3/20, or 15%
6. 34/40 or 17/20, or 85%

Warm-Up 195
1. 25
2. 25
3. 100%
4. 0%

Warm-Up 196
1. 20 times
2.–4. Answers will vary.

Warm-Up 197
1. .3 x .6 = .18 = 18%
2. .7 x .4 = .28 = 28%

Warm-Up 198
1. .2 x .15 = .03 = 3%
2. .8 x .85 = .68 = 68%

Warm-Up 199
1. 2/10 or 1/5, or 20%
2. 1/9 or about 11%
3. 2/10 x 1/9 = 1/45 = about 2%

Warm-Up 200
1. 2/20 or 1/10, or 10%
2. 1/19 or about 5%
3. 1/10 x 1/19 = 1/190 or about 0.5%

Warm-Up 201
1. 1/6 or about 17%
2. 1/6 or about 17%
3. 5/6 or about 83%

Warm-Up 202
1. 2/6 or 1/3, or 33%
2. 3/6 or 1/2, or 50%
3. 3/6 or 1/2, or 50%
4. 1/6 or about 17%

Warm-Up 203
1.

Total	Numbers
2	1 + 1
3	1 + 2
4	2 + 2, 3 + 1
5	4 + 1, 3 + 2
6	3 + 3, 4 + 2, 5 + 1
7	4 + 3, 5 + 2, 6 + 1
8	4 + 4, 5 + 3, 6 + 2
9	5 + 4, 6 + 3
10	5 + 5, 6 + 4
11	6 + 5
12	6 + 6

2. 21 total

Warm-Up 204
1. 1/21 or about 5%
2. 2/21 or about 10%
3. 3/21 or 1/7, or about 14%
4. 0/21 or 0%
5. 6, 7, and 8
6. 2, 3, 11, and 12
7. 6/21 or 2/7, or about 29%

Warm-Up 205
1. 4/52 or 1/13, or about 8%
2. 13/52 or 1/4, or about 25%
3. 1/52 or about 2%

Warm-Up 206
1. 4/49 or about 8%
2. 13/49, or about 27%

Warm-Up 207
1. D.R.
2. P.L. and F.T. by 2 inches
   F.R. and P.L. by 2 inches
   D.R. and F.R. by 2 inches
3. 51 in.
4. 14 in.

Warm-Up 208
Answers will vary.

Warm-Up 209
1. 8 in. after 3 hours
   12 in. after 4 hours
2. 34 in. after 12 hours
3. after 10 hours
4. between hours 5 and 6

Warm-Up 210
1. 2 in.
2. between days 3 and 4
3. 28 in.
4. 6 in.

Warm-Up 211
1. n = $36
2. n = $67

Warm-Up 212
1. n + $17 = $196
   n = $179
2. $17 + $13 = n
   n = $30

Warm-Up 213
1. n = 59
2. 13 + 59 – 6 = n
   n = 66

Warm-Up 214
1. n = 100 + 16 – 11 + 22
   n = 127
2. n = 100 + 16 – 11
   n = 105

Warm-Up 215
1. $80
2. $45
3. 4(20) + 3(15) = n
   n = $125

Warm-Up 216
1. $209
2. $286
3. 11(19) + 13(22) = n
   n = $495

Warm-Up 217
m = 34
d = 44

Warm-Up 218
b = 17
c = 9

Warm-Up 219
1. n = 9
2. 81
3. 3

Warm-Up 220
1. n = 1
2. 1
3. 1

Warm-Up 221
Answer = 4
4 + 4 = 8
8 is the square root of 64.

Warm-Up 222
Answer = 14
14 is the square root of 196.

Warm-Up 223
8(3) – 13 = 11
Sal's cat is 11 months old.

Warm-Up 224
16 (4) –15 = 49
Mary's dog is 49 months old. OR
Mary's dog is 4 years and 1 month old.

Warm-Up 225
n = 20

Warm-Up 226
n = 40

Warm-Up 227
1. 100/20 + 12 = 17¢
2. 100(12) – 20 = 1,180¢ or
   $11.80

Warm-Up 228
1. 20(12) + 100(12) = 1,440¢ or
   $14.40
2. 100(12) + 100(20) + 12(20) +
   28 = 3,468¢ or $34.68

Warm-Up 229

Fuel (cups)	Distance
1	3 miles
2	6 miles
3	9 miles
4	12 miles
5	15 miles
6	18 miles
7	21 miles
8	24 miles

Warm-Up 230

Fuel (cups)	Distance
1	4.5 miles
2	9 miles
3	13.5 miles
4	18 miles
5	22.5 miles
6	27 miles
7	31.5 miles
8	36 miles

Warm-Up 231
Jamie has $4.50.

Warm-Up 232
Jamie lost 1 marble.

Warm-Up 233
1. 11(-9) + 8(25) = 101
2. Ruby earned $1.01.

Warm-Up 234
1. 17(-9) + 11(25) = 122
   Ruby earned $1.22
2. 9 (-9) + 12(25) = 219
   Ruby earned $2.19

Warm-Up 235
1. (-1, -1, -2, **-3**, -5, -8, **-13**, -21,
   -34, -55, -89, **-144**, **-233**)
2. Add two consecutive numbers
   to get the next number.

Warm-Up 236
(-144, -233, -377, **-610**, -987,
-1597, **-2584**)

Warm-Up 237
23(.10) + 44(.05) + 51(.25) =
$17.25

Warm-Up 238
23(1) + 5(5) + 4(10) = $88

Warm-Up 239
$206

Warm-Up 240
$89

Warm-Up 241
6 tickets

Warm-Up 242
1. 46 tickets
2. $11.50

Warm-Up 243
201 stickers

Warm-Up 244
147 baseball cards

Warm-Up 245
1. y = $10 – (.67 x 6)
2. y = $5.98

Warm-Up 246
1. n = (12 x 6) – 4
2. n = 68 candies

Warm-Up 247
1. y + 2k + 8m = n
2. 1 + 2(2) + 8(3) = 29

Warm-Up 248
1. 3m + y + 3k = n
2. 3(3) + (1) + 3(2) = 16

Warm-Up 249

Ounces	Cost
1	$0.44
2	$0.88
3	$1.32
4	$1.76
5	$2.20
6	$2.64
7	$3.08
8	$3.52
9	$3.96
10	$4.40

2. $4.84
3. $5.28

Warm-Up 250

Ounces	Cost
1	$0.47
2	$0.94
3	$1.41
4	$1.88
5	$2.35
6	$2.82
7	$3.29
8	$3.76
9	$4.23
10	$4.70
11	$5.17
12	$5.64

2. $2.35
3. $4.23
4. $5.64